Salvation, the Baptism in the Holy Spirit, and the Gift of Tongues

A PERSONAL JOURNEY AND
SCRIPTURAL DISCUSSION

Michael L. Davis

TRILOGY CHRISTIAN PUBLISHERS
Tustin, CA

Trilogy Christian Publishers
A Wholly Owned Subsidiary of Trinity Broadcasting Network
2442 Michelle Drive
Tustin, CA 92780

Salvation, the Baptism in the Holy Spirit, and the Gift of Tongues
Copyright © 2023 by Michael L. Davis

Scripture quotations marked AMP are taken from the Amplified® Bible (AMP), Copyright © 2015 by The Lockman Foundation. Used by permission. www.Lockman.org.

Scripture quotations marked ESV are taken from the ESV® Bible (The Holy Bible, English Standard Version®), copyright © 2001 by Crossway Bibles, a publishing ministry of Good News Publishers. Used by permission. All rights reserved.

Scripture quotations marked NKJV are taken from the New King James Version®. Copyright © 1982 by Thomas Nelson. Used by permission. All rights reserved.

Scripture quotations marked NASB are taken from the New American Standard Bible® (NASB), Copyright © 1977 by The Lockman Foundation. Used by permission. www.Lockman.org.

No part of this book may be reproduced, stored in a retrieval system, or transmitted by any means without written permission from the author. All rights reserved. Printed in the USA.

Rights Department, 2442 Michelle Drive, Tustin, CA 92780.

Trilogy Christian Publishing/TBN and colophon are trademarks of Trinity Broadcasting Network.

Cover design by Jeff Summers

For information about special discounts for bulk purchases, please contact Trilogy Christian Publishing.

Trilogy Disclaimer: The views and content expressed in this book are those of the author and may not necessarily reflect the views and doctrine of Trilogy Christian Publishing or the Trinity Broadcasting Network.

Manufactured in the United States of America

10 9 8 7 6 5 4 3 2 1

Library of Congress Cataloging-in-Publication Data is available.

ISBN: 979-8-88738-308-8

E-ISBN: 979-8-88738-309-5 (ebook)

Dedication

Among the body of Christ, I do not think there has been an issue as controversial and divisive as the topic of salvation and its relationship with the baptism in the Holy Spirit, spiritual gifts, and the gift of tongues. The important thing to remember is that there are brothers and sisters on both sides of this issue that are born again, love the Lord, and whose heart desire is to live their Christian walk according to what they believe the Bible teaches. Remembering that is paramount. Unfortunately, at times, discussions turn into disagreements, which turn into arguments, and another wedge is driven into the body of Christ. And, of course, the whole time, either side feels they are defending the Word, coming against error, and trying to protect what they feel to be true. And in many ways, that is honorable—for all sides. It shows our care and concern for the Word of God. But we need to remember that the issue here is

Jesus and how we can serve Him and share Him with a person, city, or world that does not know Him.

This book is dedicated to groups of friends with whom, over the years, we have had many marvelous discussions on an assorted array of spiritual topics. On this particular topic, however, we disagree. This is the wonderful thing about being brothers and sisters in the body of Christ. It reminds me of the scripture that says, "One Lord, one faith, one baptism" (Ephesians 4:5, NASB). The bottom line of it all is that we are one in Christ.

To my wife, Kimberly. Thank You, Lord, for choosing her to be my partner for life. I can only pray that I can be as good of a husband to her as she is a wife to me.

Also, to my friend and forever pastor, John Vick, past senior pastor of the First Foursquare Church of Jacksonville, Florida. Through his ministry, our family has been challenged and grown in so many spiritual ways. We love our church.

But first and foremost, to my Lord and Savior, Jesus Christ. As a fourteen-year-old boy in 1974, He spoke to my heart and gave me eternal life. As a young adult, early in 1983, He spoke to my heart again and baptized me in the Holy Spirit. Thank You, Lord.

May miracles never cease.

Dedicated to Brandon, Mikayla, and Jason. May each of you actually read this and be blessed by it one day.

About the Front Cover

This image describes us all in our journey as we walk out our faith. Here we have the cross, which is placed in a seemingly darkened barren valley. This dark and barren valley represents us in a time before we knew Christ or gave our lives to Him. The cross represents the finished work of Christ, His suffering for us, and His offering of salvation. The cross itself is being transformed into the image of the dove, which is the Holy Spirit going forth into the world seeking to be poured out upon us. Jesus said the Helper (Holy Spirit) could not come unless He went away. Christ is no longer on the cross, and we have the Holy Spirit. It is Jesus Christ who baptizes us in the Holy Spirit after we come to the cross to receive salvation. It is the Holy Spirit who fills us. At the bottom left, far off in the distance, is the figure of an individual, walking in the valley of his or her life, for they have not yet come to the cross, but they will, for the Holy Spirit calls to them. The subdued colors of the light and darkness are reminiscent of where we were before Christ but behold, a better day is coming, for the kingdom of heaven is at hand.

Contents

Foreword ix
Preface xi
Chapter 1. 1
    Beginnings 1
Chapter 2. 16
    And So It Begins 16
Chapter 3. 28
    Let's Go! 28
Chapter 4. 40
    John the Baptist Announces a New Era 40
    What It is to Be Born Again 47
Chapter 5. 70
    Okay, but What about This "Baptism in the Holy Spirit" and "Tongues" Stuff? 70
    Sidebar on the Role of the Holy Spirit 73
    Back to the Baptism in the Holy Spirit 74
    Have You Been to Samaria Lately? 79
    Be All You Can Be 82
    Saul…I Mean, Paul 87
Chapter 6. 93
    Let's Dig a Little Deeper 93
Chapter 7. 108
    So, Where Do We Go From Here? 108

Could We Use a Little Armor Over Here? 116
Something for You to Think About 119
Is Your Relationship with God a River or a Well? . 120
Chapter 8. 125
   A Little Recap with Some Q and A 125
Chapter 9. 149
   The Preeminence of Jesus Christ and the Bible....149
   Pontius Pilate and the Scapegoat 154
   The Washing of Hands 157
   Old Times/New Times Converge 159
   But We Must Beware the Leaven 165
   Enter the Cohanim 166
   The Hidden Beauty of Hyssop 171
   Cleansing and Forgiveness of Sin..................... 172
   First Fruits, Feast Days, and Jesus Christ 176
   The Tamid 178
   The Feast of the Fiftieth Day 180
   The New Covenant and Substitutionary Sacrifice ..183
   The Cockcrow 192
A Few Last Thoughts 196
About the Author.. 203
Endnotes 204

Foreword

Mike Davis and I have known each other since the 1990s. Our meeting was a moment of providence wrapped in a cloud of mystery. It was one of those encounters that made it seem like every step we had taken prior really was with the intention of bringing us to a meeting. Mike's wife, Kim, had set an appointment for Mike to meet with me because the denomination to which I belonged had a meaningful impact on his earlier life. Unknown to either of us, he was going to cancel the meeting until, by chance, he encountered my wife, Shawn, at a Home Depot and asked her about the Foursquare shirt she was wearing. By no other explanation than the Holy Spirit, my wife looked up, and the first thing she said was, "Aren't you supposed to meet with my husband this week?"

Needless to say, he did not cancel the meeting, and we have been a steadfast part of each other's lives ever since.

Mike is someone who is deeply touched by the many spiritual moments that oftentimes go unnoticed by most people. Whether it is divine appointments, prayer with a stranger, baptism, communion, or baptism of the Holy Spirit, Mike is someone who doesn't see the act as some passive event but rather a cosmic-shifting event.

Mike shared the guts of what has become this book years ago. I cannot think of anyone I would rather tell the story of the power of the Holy Spirit and the incredible gift this is as our prayer language.

Mike, Kim, Mikayla, and Jason are a part of the fabric of my family's story, and I thank God for the little moments that lead to this moment.

John Vick.
December 11, 2021.

Preface

This book has been a labor of love for the past forty years. The seeds of it were first planted around 1984 during my first enlistment with the United States Air Force, stationed in Great Falls, Montana. While there, I met several Christians from varying denominations, and we saw each other as brothers and were very close friends. Some of us were doctrinal opposites on a few things, this topic being one of them. One of my friends "dared" me to read a book by John F. MacArthur, Jr called *The Charismatics*. He was sure that after reading that book, I would be straightened out. Well, I did read the book, I took notes on the book, highlighted parts, and I enjoyed the book, but the only thing the book did was convince me more of my position. I tried to discuss the outline with my friend, but he wasn't interested in having the discussion, which I felt was unfortunate. So, I sort of started outlining some notes about this and tucked it away.

The next seed occurred in the mid-1990s when I was listening to a Christian AM radio station and heard a message from one of the most influential pastors of one of the largest churches in the city. I loved listening to his teaching; he was solid, a phenomenal speaker, and had done incredible things for the kingdom of God. I trusted him, and he was one of my favorites. But on this particular day, the message was very much against my belief in the use of spiritual gifts, especially my stance on what we call baptism in the Holy Spirit. I was glued to the radio, taking in every word, then called the church and ordered the tape. Since I was aware of his denomination, I already knew that he would be opposed to this, but to hear him preach against it somehow made it different. I sort of became indignant.

And the thought kept going through my head, *How could I, a "nobody nothing," not line up with his message?* He was the preacher of a 10,000-plus congregation, a renowned church, had all the education, all the knowledge, all the influence, and here I am saying that his position is wrong. How does that make sense? And then, over time, I came to the realization that there are great preachers and famous pastors on both sides of this topic.

And this was also when I learned something else about myself: The difference between belief and conviction.

Someone will say to me, "Well, that is your belief," or "That is what you believe."

I will say, "No, that is my conviction."

A belief is malleable; a conviction is not.

There are no gray areas with a conviction.

Take, for example, a topic on something the Christian church likes to go round and round with, a topic like, say, "the rapture." You can be a pre-tribulationist, a mid-tribulation believer, a post-tribulation type, or any of the other positions. In fact, you can even be none of those, and it would not change a thing. The Christian world runs the gamut on these positions, some very strongly, but at the end of the day, these are all beliefs; they could be right or could be wrong. A belief is simply a little stronger than an opinion.

*But...*Jesus Christ, the Son of God, who is God in the flesh, eternal, born of a virgin, fully God, fully man, He died for our sins, He rose from the dead, eternal salvation is through Him, in His name, He will return for His church, and through Him, the world will be judged—this is a conviction...it is not malleable and has no gray area.

This is much stronger than a belief or an opinion. This is the truth.

For me, the topic of this book is more than a belief; it is a conviction.

Because of this view, I have never been afraid of opposing views; in fact, I welcome them. I love to hear the opposite side as long as someone is willing to have an honest discourse. The book I was challenged to read did not intimidate me; it spurred me on. The message from the megachurch did not threaten my stance; it compelled me to dig deeper, study more, and through that, I became stronger. So, I started to do an outline, studying, researching, taking notes, and finally put it to paper. It has been a fantastic journey, and the result is what you have before you.

The purpose of this book is to bring understanding to the topic concerning baptism in the Holy Spirit. Jestingly, there are generally two schools of thought on this: the "yeses" and the "nos." There is a smaller third camp called the "I'm not sures." This book is intended for all three groups. But even if you were not convinced otherwise, I would hope that this would at least help you to understand from a biblical perspective and gain an understanding of why we believe and worship the way we do. If you are in the "I'm not sure" camp, I hope this discussion will present to you convincing scriptural reasons why you should be sure.

I fully understand why some people and denominations do not agree with this doctrine. I would like to build some bridges and share with you from the scriptures why there are some that do. Throughout my Christian life, I have read and studied many books and listened to several teachings about why we have it wrong.

You may have a few of them on your bookshelf. Some were very enjoyable, even though I disagreed with their position. But it taught me a couple of things: to study, to seek God, and finally, to know why I believe what I believe. And that is what I would like for you to do.

Another thing it has taught me is this: Just because a popular pastor or evangelist is for or against a certain position, including my own, that is not the basis for anyone to form his or her beliefs. You can learn from all of them, but let the Bible be your basis. Being on television or writing a hundred books does not make one infallible. There are just as many great and truly respected men of God on one side of this issue as there are on the other.

So, let's discuss this topic together, and upfront, I will tell you that it will be from a person who definitely believes in the blessing of salvation through Jesus Christ, the baptism in the Holy Spirit, and spiritual gifts; in this case, the evidence of speaking or praying in tongues. I would like to share with you why. All I would ask is that you would read this prayerfully, use your Bible for the scripture references, and read objectively. It is written in a discussion format and was fun to write. And if a point is brought up that suddenly gets your attention, or something is presented in a way in which you have not previously thought about before, then think about it. Don't just pass it off. If something in here raises questions for you because you have been taught differently, but now this seems to make a little more sense, ask yourself why that is. Find the answers to your unanswered questions. Pray about them. And if you disagree with what is in this book, then have a valid scriptural reason as to why it is that you disagree. Don't just say, "Well, I don't believe that," or, "My preacher says it is wrong." Find out from the Bible why it is that you don't believe that. Think about them. And if you are a Christian but have never paid much attention to matters like this, perhaps this book will quicken your interest. It is important that you use your Bible and follow along as you read this. Don't just read this pile of paper. Go to the scripture references. That way, we can stay together. Highlight, underline, and cross-reference. Take notes. Pray and think about things. And have fun. This can really be fun.

Chapter 1

Beginnings

As far back as I can remember, I have always loved learning about and studying the Word of God. I was fascinated by the Bible, its make-up, authors, history, and its transmittal through time. I still am. To be sure, I was raised in a Christian home but not in an overtly religious family. Sort of an eclectic mixture of Baptist (my dad) and Catholic (my mom), but at the time, neither was religiously rigid in practice.

I had an idyllic childhood; loving nurturing parents, a great dad, a great mom, and two awesome sisters, same with my grandparents on both sides, all of whom shared the values of hard work and respect for others, especially for adults and elders. I could not have had a better childhood. It was the traditional home life of a dad who worked with a mom at home.

And I was raised with a healthy respect for God.

As I grew older, it was instilled in me that you always respected God and the things of God, even if your actual life said otherwise—because while no one is perfect in practice, your intentions should be. You slightly bowed your head at the name of Jesus, you didn't slam the Bible down on the counter, nor did you ever put anything on top of the Bible. God and the things of God were holy and to be respected. One of my earliest memories as a little kid, somewhere around first grade, after watching an old black and white movie of St. Francis of Assisi, I then went to my room, stood on my bed, and stretched out my arms against the wall and prayed for the same experience as portrayed in the movie (the stigmata). At six or seven years old, I really wanted this and asked God to do it for me. As a teenager, running with my friends and doing things that teenagers do—but shouldn't be doing, I would sometimes think of the words of my grandfather, who told me when I was little, "Don't ever use God's name in vain because when you really need Him, and you call on Him, He might think you were only kidding." Wise words from a grandfather to a small boy, which stuck with me through the years. For me, that cuss word was off-limits. For these reasons, whatever season I was in growing up, I always had a deep respect for God, even if you couldn't tell from the outside.

Like most parents, they made us go to church when we were little; then, as time went by, they got tired of the battle, and church mostly went by the wayside. We moved a lot every few years, which did not help a lot (thank you, United States Air Force). In twelve years of school, I was in probably eight different schools, the life of a military family.

But they believed in God, they absolutely believed in the atoning work of Jesus Christ, whatever life would bring, and they made sure we were raised with that knowledge.

As time passed, my dad retired, both parents embarked on their new phase of life, both went back to work, and seasons of change began to flow. Life was different. Home was different. Starting out in a not-so-nice neighborhood and, about a year later, moved into a nicer neighborhood. But life had changed. With three teenage kids at home, both Mom and Dad working on running a household, out of necessity, we became latchkey kids, and parental oversight and involvement waned in our formative teenage years.

Then in 1974, at about fourteen years old, a friend down the road invited me to church. We went to school together and sometimes hung out together, and his father was the minister of music at Evangel Temple Assembly of God. They were having a special music guest, and that night, I learned what it was to be born again. The experience of sitting in that church pew and answering that call is something I will never forget. I went forward and asked Jesus to come into my heart to be my Lord and Savior. I meant every word, and I had to tell everybody. My dad was elated, and my mom, well, she was okay with it but kind of suspect because the experience was not Catholic, but I didn't care because, man, I was saved, and I knew it. There was no one happier on the face of the earth.

As time went on, like most teenagers, I fully embraced the teenager experience. New things had become important, and any thoughts of God left me as other things took His place.

This is a difficult time because, looking back, I see myself as if standing on the sidelines, watching things slowly disintegrate. I could see Mom and Dad growing more separate and following the path of least resistance, and so did I. So did all of us.

The phenomenal thing is that I was not the only one on the sidelines; so was God. The awesome thing is, He never leaves or forsakes you—any of us. God was on the sidelines with me, patiently waiting. I had earlier called out to Him, and He answered. When I walked away to discover new things, He let me, but He never took His eyes off of me. I can see now He was watching. He waits for us. And He gives prompts to let us know He is there and that He waits for us. There were prompts all through this time in my life. It was my decision to live and go about life the way I was; I can just see Him saying, "Okay, Mike, how much more? How far do you want to go?"

A few years went by when, through another friend, I visited a small country church called Fleming Island Baptist Church. I fell in love with the Reverend Paul Estes, who impacted me more than he will ever know. I loved this man; he exemplified such grace and compassion. But man, he was non-apologetic when it came to the gospel. While there, it struck me that there was a preacher whose sixteen-year-old daughter had been abducted and murdered just a few years earlier, and for whatever he and his family went through during this time, he remained faithful to his calling. I was the same age as his daughter Janita; we went to the same school, although I did not personally know her. Even though I had heard about what had happened (everyone had), I did not know he was the preacher or that she was his daughter when I visited his church. What I did hear was the gospel. I answered the call, joined the church, rededicated my life, and was baptized. I was there for about a year or so, brought some friends from time to time, and my dad even went with me on occasion. I was moving a little more from the sidelines.

But I eventually quit attending—because, well, there were other things to explore. Or so I thought. This was the slide when things slowly began to unravel, not overnight, but little by little, decision by decision, even when God was trying to get my attention.

Another prompt, after I had slid further away, was when a friend gave me a small paperback book. The thought was nice, and I appreciated it, but it was a religious book, and it found its way to the closet. Looking back, I can see prompts and little reminders that God was still in the mix. Something said, something done, some interaction that would turn my thoughts to Him. It is absolutely true that once you have been graced/touched/indwelt by the Holy Spirit after being born again, He is always present with you—even if you are not present with Him. He is still speaking, even when you are not listening. I still had the underlying respect, but my life was a mess. In my second year of college, I even took a "Bible as literature" class in which I chose the book of Isaiah as my literary research paper, and chose it because it was such a large book in the Bible. It fascinated me, and I soaked it up. That was a good prompt, but I was still exploring and sort of resumed my previous life, literally sinking further into nothingness, experimenting with things in which I knew better, mostly a constant variety of recreational drugs and, of course, my fair share of alcohol. In fact, at the time, I think that was my main goal in life because then I did not have to think, worry, or deal with the life in which I was miserably failing. But the use was constant, and if I couldn't go to school with my stash, I didn't want to go to school. Of course, I was having fun...outwardly.

Young, carefree, and had no real responsibilities except showing up for work, chasing all of the fun I could find with people who wanted to have the same fun I was having. But I was getting older now, just over twenty years old, still living at home, using school as an excuse, and I was facing the realities of life.

The gig was up.

I was going nowhere, and I knew it. I was living in a fractured home, which certainly did not help to make things any better. Working part-time at night, I had no direction, no goals in life, paying my way to go on and off to the local junior college, of which I had no goal there either and did horribly. It was like spinning your tires in the sand until you run out of gas.

Then the day came when my mom asked me how I would feel if she and Dad got a divorce. I was fine with it. I was roughly nineteen or twenty years old at the time, and I met and answered the question without emotion. I loved my mom, and I loved my dad immensely, just not together. Everyone was living their own lives anyway, and I was no different. It was no big deal, and I wanted whatever was best for them. I knew they had each given their all in this thing called life; they were great parents, actually phenomenal parents who showered us with love and sacrificed their entire life all these years until slowly, over time, life became overwhelming. They had given enough; to each other, the kids, and to everyone else. It took a few years for the divorce to take place, but it eventually happened. They had married young, raised three kids, constantly moved, and never settled in one place until Dad retired from the military. They never fought or argued that I saw; they just grew very separate. It was time to move on. There was a time when I had so little interaction with my parents that I didn't feel I even knew them anymore, and I was sure they did not know me. Not the real me. I never saw it as their fault or my fault; it was just life. Even though we were all under the same roof, we all lived apart. I did the same.

I was a mess, my life was a mess, and my future was more of a mess. There was absolutely no direction or purpose in anything. Drugs to escape reality had become a reality.

I became fascinated by the evil portrayed in rock and roll lyrics, backmasking in music, and symbols on the albums; not agreeing with it, just fascinated with it. Bought a book, The Satanic Bible, by (I don't even want to print his name), but you can see him peering through the top balcony in the Eagles' Hotel California album. Also read through a book called The Urantia Book while searching for whatever I was searching for. I learned about this because Kerry Livgren of the rock group Kansas was a follower, and he was obviously successful, so maybe I could follow this and be successful too. But it was all evil, and I knew it was evil, but I was fascinated with all of it, and it went with the lifestyle that I was living.

Then late one night in 1982, while driving across the Buckman Bridge coming home from work while smoking PCP-laced pot to drown out my reality, I am looking at the road, and as I look to the outside of my little Datsun King Cab, it appears that I am doing about thirty miles per hour. The speedometer said seventy, but the road said differently. The bridge said differently. Looking out the window, everything was in slow motion. I got to thinking, *What if I turned into the side of the bridge, it would be like a slow-motion crunch, and I would have plenty of time to get out and not be hurt.* I really wanted to do it. I somehow wanted to experience this slow crunch into the bridge, and I was considering it when I suddenly felt my left wrist twitch on the steering wheel to break hard left into the bridge. I didn't turn the wheel, but I felt my hand on the steering wheel twitch in that direction.

Then late one night, having sunk below the depths of where I had previously been, I cried out. Very literally cried out. Broken, lost, with real tears. I cried out to God.

I had had enough. I remember coming home from work one night; it was a little before midnight, I was stoned when I walked into work, and I continued that process on the drive home from work and continued still when I sat down in the house. Various drugs were very important to me because they seemed to be the only reality I could cling to. Pot, hash, Quaaludes, PCP—my parents knew I was doing some things but had no idea of what or how much. In fact, I used to grow plants in the house. I was incredibly unhappy inside—and angry. Angry at my lot in life, angry at my lack of direction, angry at the family breakdown, angry at being completely lost, angry at not being able to do anything about it, angry at life, and angry at God. I was raised right, knew right from wrong, good from bad, and I should be better than this.

So, I did what any good stoner would do in a situation like this; I blamed God.

Yes, I still believed in God. The reality of God was never a question. Where I was in life was a question, but His existence was a given. I had seen the evil, and if there was evil, which is associated with satan, then there must be good, which is associated with God. It made perfect rational sense. However, since God is God, and me not being one to take responsibility for my own actions or decisions, I blamed Him.

I can still relive it now; I came home one evening from work, my parents were hopefully asleep in the back bedroom, I piled up in the recliner in the great room, sparked up a bowl to continue my state of blurriness, and I really laid it on Him. This was all His fault; I was so justified in taking it out on Him.

"What are You doing?" "How could You do this?" "Look at my mess of a life; it is not right! This is so unfair," "I am going nowhere," calling Him out, justifying my lot with all of these rationalized questions. And I remember saying, "Come on, God, speak to me...help me...I don't know what to do." And actual tears started to flow.

I was broken, wallowing in self-pity, and literally wishing I had never been born.

The date was September 26, 1982. Twelve fifteen in the morning.

And then...here it comes...a prompt.

Sitting there wallowing and feeling sorry for myself, I looked at the bookshelf next to the chair. Laying there on top of some other books was a HarperCollins Study Bible that my parents had given to me a little more than two years before on my twentieth birthday. I had used the book, studied from it, read parts of it, and did my college Isaiah report from it, this book was familiar, but now I knew it not.

I picked up the book, sat back down, closed my eyes, literally simply flipped it open, pointed my finger, and it landed on Jeremiah 7:8–10: (This was God speaking to me)

> Behold, you trust in deceptive words to no avail. Will you steal, murder, commit adul-

tery, swear falsely, burn incense to Baal, and go after other gods that you have not known, and then come and stand before me in this house, which is called by my name, and say 'We are delivered!'—only to go on doing all these abominations?

It was like being struck by a bolt of lightning; I could not believe what I was reading.

"Behold, you trust in deceptive words to no avail," which is exactly what I was doing with the rationalized questions and everything I was blaming Him for.

"Will you steal, murder, commit adultery, swear falsely, burn incense to Baal."

Everything on this list I was guilty of, minus the murder; everything else was me with a target, including burning incense to Baal because that is the smoke, the incense, and the aroma from the drugs with which I was approaching Him. Baal, whose name means "lord," "master," or "possessor," was the Phoenician god by which sacrifices were made, including human sacrifices, incense burned, and worshiped as lord. Baal worship represented the epitome of immorality, where they practiced their religion with their own priests, temples, and altars. To participate in Baal worship was expressly forbidden by the true God and man; this was *me*. Incense to Baal was the same as smoking pot. God was talking to me.

"And then come and stand before me in this house ... only to go on doing all of these abominations?"

"And then come before me." Just wow. That hit me hard. How could I? How dare I come before Him in this condition with this attitude; my life was an abomination, and I had no plans to cease anytime soon. I thought I could approach the Holy in this way? Wow, the gig really was up. He was having none of it. The reference, by the way, is Jeremiah 7, beginning with verse 8. It was a divine act; this was me exactly at this very point in time. I had literally closed my eyes, opened the Bible, and blindly pointed to this verse. God was listening, God was speaking to me, God answered my prayer, and what's more, I knew God was chastising me. The creator of the universe was not feeling sorry for me. He knew that I knew better, that I was raised better. He knew that I had created this situation, and He knew that at one point, and on occasions after that, I had invited Him to be Lord of my life. He knew this stuff, but He was simply waiting for me. Waiting for me to run it all out, waiting on me to quit being stupid. Funny thing about free will...it is free will. But the thing that got to me most was this: *He had heard, and He had answered.* I was actually glad to hear from Him, even if it wasn't for hugs and a mutual pity party.

And what's more, I had come to Him with all of these questions, which by definition required an answer, and if you will notice, He ended His sentence with a question to me—which also required an answer. From me.

In short, His question was this, "Mike, what right do you think you have that can come to Me in this way, defaming the holy, doing all of these abominations, living the way you are, doing what you are doing, of which you know better and think I am going to deliver you? And you want to blame your lot in life on *Me*?" That is what I heard.

I was not nine years old anymore. I was a twenty-two-year-old full-grown brat living like hell. Later on, one thing my wife and I taught our own kids when they were little was this: You are right now covered by the faith of your parents (we prayed over and anointed our kids every evening before bed), but there will come a day when you will have your own relationship with God, and you will be responsible for your own walk with Him. At twenty-two years old, this was on me.

September 26, 1982, was the night that began to change the direction of my life. I knew God had spoken to me; I knew He had asked a question and that the next move was on me.

I know the date because such was the impact that that very night, I wrote the date and time in that HarperCollins Study Bible. The funny thing is, I had already underlined that very same verse about two years before. It was a prompt that I missed—or didn't want to see—

or didn't care about. He was reaching out to me even back then. I was not going to miss it this time. It was time to get off the sidelines.

Chapter 2

And So It Begins

This was a private personal thing between God and me, I didn't make any big pronouncements, home was the same. I simply quietly took stock of where I was and what had happened. I repented, and I surrendered.

Over the next several months, I started making changes in my own life. I quit all drugs and alcohol cold turkey, cleaned out my truck, and got rid of anything that I perceived to be contrary to my new direction and commitment. I mowed the lawn. I was clean, felt clean, and wanted everything around me to be clean. This included music, certain clothes, paraphernalia, and books; it didn't matter. Anything reminiscent of the old "me" was off the table, including some friends.

And I remember very distinctly when I saw my mom, I hugged her and told her that I loved her, and when I saw my dad, I did the same.

I quietly started reading the Bible, focusing on the New Testament because I wanted to learn everything I could about the person and life of Jesus Christ. I bought a dedicated notepad and started to outline the Gospels chapter by chapter. I felt like a dry sponge dropped into a bucket of water. Remember that book given to me by a friend that I had tossed into the closet about two years earlier? It was that prompt that I ignored. I dug out the book, noticed for the first time there was a personal inscription on the inside cover from the friend who had given it to me, and began to read. The book was called *How to Live Like a King's Kid* by a guy named Harold Hill. I loved this book and still love it today. I connected with this guy, his experiences, and his humor. I liked his simplistic approach to faith, and it was the perfect starting point for me. I needed simple.

Other books that had an impact on me during this time, among others, were *How to Be a Christian Without Being Religious* by Fritz Ridenour, *Celebration of Discipline* by Richard Foster, and *A Handbook for New Charismatics* by Warren Thwing.

I learned a lot from reading and researching, and I found an AM radio station that had preachers on all day; it quickly became my favorite station. Remember, this was in the early 80s; there was no internet, social media, or outlets like that. Cassette tapes and the U. S. Mail ruled the day. And I started to learn things...

I was getting pretty good at referencing things from which I was reading or listening to with my Bible. And I prayed a lot. I was learning about a new kind of prayer—new to me—called praying in the Spirit. It was referenced in the *King's Kid* book I had read and certain preachers that I listened to on the radio. I had never heard of this before and had to go to the Scriptures to research. And there it was; the book of Acts, 1 Corinthians, Ephesians, the book of Jude...I began to think I was the only one who was not aware of this. I was also learning some new terms, like "baptism in the Holy Spirit," "praying in tongues," and "gifts of the Spirit," things I had never heard of before. I was so simplistic and naïve when it came to my new faith; I naturally thought everybody would be on board with anything that I was on board with concerning Jesus. Well, and I am sitting here smiling, I shortly found out that was not the case.

So, for a couple of months, although I was still working at night, during the day, instead of doing drugs and the like, I was riding around in my truck, listening to preachers, and studying the Word. I was learning so much, and God was bringing into my path others of like faith and commitment. One thing about druggie friends, when you quit doing what they are doing, they don't want you around as part of their secret society anymore. You are no longer cool if you are not helping to provide the stash that helps to keep everybody going.

It worked out great for me because I was in a season of learning and strengthening my own faith. This is where I wanted to be—except I wanted to learn more about this other baptism stuff. I wanted to learn about anything that would give me a deeper relationship with Jesus Christ. I learned about fasting, prayer, and other disciplines and read some amazing books, but I mostly fell back in love with the Bible. It was a new book in a new world. God kept bringing people in my path that knew about or had experienced this baptism in the Holy Spirit that is talked about in the Gospels and epistles. I had learned there were churches that believed in this and those that did not. I also learned that when it came to certain doctrines, all was not so harmonious in the Christian land. Even though I had received Jesus Christ when I was fourteen years old and had an on-and-off commitment to the faith in the years following, I was basically a new Christian, at least a new, fully committed Christian. To phrase it perfectly, I felt like I was "born again." It was fortunate that I did not have a lot of baggage to deal with on the "religious" side; all of my baggage was from the world. In my Eclectic Catholic/Protestant mix of upbringing, I had learned the surface tenants of serving God, going to church, Sunday school, CCD, and the normal religious things people do, but I did not have a lot of doctrinal hurdles to get over. I didn't really care about denominations; I was basically starting out from scratch—which was a good thing. This actually made things easier as I simply took the Bible, read what was written, and believed what it said. I had come to the realization, based on my study of the Bible, prayer, and what I was experiencing from a spiritual perspective, that this was for real. I was older now, forming my own relationship with God as He was leading; I was in my training season, my proving ground, and I wanted more. I wanted to go beyond the religiousness of being a "Christian," I wanted to serve God with every fiber of my being. I prayed in earnest; I prayed to receive all He had for me.

A slight pause here. You think this is all about me; it is not.

It is about you. Where are you on your journey?

My spiritual experience and upbringing are not atypical of many of you reading this book, and my journey is no more or less special than yours is. This is simply my story, open and honest. You have your own personal story in your walk with God, your own prompts, your own experiences, and your own leadings. I would highly encourage you to write it down. Most of us have some background in some type of church, off-and-on fellowships throughout our lives, and defining experiences that God had in store for each of us to bring us to a certain place at a particular time in our lives. Some of these events were right before our faces; some look back and see the hand of God working. But they are there, nonetheless.

And some of you may not have had these experiences, live events, or divine appointments. Maybe you had a completely different journey, maybe you were raised with no spiritual interest at all, never stepped foot in a church, and maybe He revealed Himself to you in a completely different way. But reveal to you He has.

So...at the end of the day, it does not matter. We are all unique in God's eyes, special; He created each of us for Him for His purpose. We all have a unique journey. However, what does matter is this: how much we embraced that journey, recognized the prompts, or follow the leading of the Holy Spirit is entirely up to us; the many times we went one way when we knew to go the other. And quite honestly, this journey lasts our entire lifetime. You never "arrive" or are "finished" because God is never finished until He takes us home. We can accept, or we can reject. And believe this—God will continue to bring us to Him, even in the times we reject, and if I have proved anything, it is this—that God is patient.

I had the best parents in the world, and a perfect childhood, up to about a six or seven-year window where I fell off the ledge. That falling was totally on me. I am responsible, I turned away, it was my conscious decision, the choices that I made, the people I associated with, and the activities that I chose to engage in. It was on me. And the deeper I fell, the more content I was to wallow in it. Until, like the story of the prodigal son, I "came to my senses." It really was a point of desperation. I had to get back to God, and I had to do one thing...

Repent.

And so I did. That night on September 26, 1982, when I cracked open the Bible and God hit me with that verse from Jeremiah chapter 7, I knew God was speaking to me. I was not going to let this one pass. For me, it might be the last time.

That night, I changed my direction.

For several months, I purposed to follow God wherever He led me. I prayed, studied, researched, prayed, studied, fasted, and then, to top it all off, I prayed and studied. As hard as I had worked to be rebellious, I worked doubly hard to be obedient.

It was about a five-month period of proving ground, and looking back, I now know that even though God knows the end from the beginning, sometimes we go through things so we can prove to ourselves where we are. Sometimes we need to know. Much like Abraham when he offered up Isaac on the altar. Abraham was coming down with the knife to sacrifice his son until God stopped him with an angel. Abraham needed to know his commitment; God already knew.

SALVATION, THE BAPTISM IN THE HOLY SPIRIT, AND THE GIFT OF TONGUES

I believe in God; I believe in heaven, hell, angels, and demons; that there is good and there is evil. And I always have. I believe there is a spiritual dimension and a spiritual dynamic to everything about us. I think that if we could see into that realm, much like Elijah did, we would be amazed. And I believe we, as both physical and spiritual beings, can be influenced spiritually for either good or bad, which we act out in the physical.

I also believe satan is real and that he does not like to give up his property very easily. There were a couple of experiences in this five-month period that will stick with me for the rest of my life. Although the intent was probably to keep me away from my new commitment, the end result was that it drove me closer to the arms of Jesus and to the safety of God.

I hesitated in writing this, but after prayerful consideration, I included it because not only is it verily, verily true, it is part of the journey that solidified my determination to serve Jesus Christ. The first occurrence took place not long, maybe a month or two after I had recommitted my life to Christ. I was asleep in bed and what woke me up (and I do mean fully awake) was the very sense of a very real presence of evil in my room, standing next to the bed, looking down on me. I felt evil incarnate, and it startled me. I could not move. I could not speak. I was literally paralyzed. The most I could do was squirm; my legs could not move; they felt as if they were in quicksand or up to my hips in thick mud. I had never felt fear to this degree, but I was scared and too paralyzed by fear to move. It was surreal, but it was real. I tried to speak out but could not talk. I could open my mouth, but my tongue would not move, and it felt as if it was swollen twice its size. There was this very presence of evil standing next to me in my room, and it truly felt like satan himself. And I know I already said this once, but to emphasize, I felt incredible fear. In my mind, I started calling on Jesus and calling on the blood of Jesus. I kept saying "Jesus, Jesus, Jesus..." over and over and "blood of Jesus, blood of Jesus" in my mind, and the presence left. I knew—I could tell exactly when the evil presence left. It vanished with the repeated name of Jesus, and when it left, my body was loosed and back to normal. I know there are sleep studies and so-called scientific explanations for what happened because I have read them. And while I am grateful for all of our doctors, knowledge, and learning of our medical professionals, I also know what it was.

It was the very presence of evil. And it was in my room. This type of experience has happened twice in my life, once here and once the exact same way, several years later. Another occurrence took place not long after, when one evening, I was alone in my room, kneeling at the foot of the bed, down on both knees...praying. I was literally praying. I am not here to get into a theological debate about what happened or what this means; I am just reporting what took place. I was at the foot of the bed, on both knees, with my head bowed and resting on the foot of the bed. I was praying to God and focused on God. What happened next was so quick, and I have trouble describing it in words. I very suddenly sensed that same evil presence right behind me, as if towering over the back of my shoulder. I sensed seething hate and anger, and as soon as I sensed it, I was suddenly struck and knocked straight down to the floor. That is the best way I can describe it. It was like a downward explosion. As if someone had put both of their hands together over their head and hit me between the shoulder blades—like I had been hit from behind and knocked straight down. There was no physical contact, nothing physically hit me, but there is no other way to describe it. It was just a power, a force, that suddenly came down on me, and I found myself on the carpet. And then it was gone—everything, the sense of evil, hate, and anger. It was gone. This whole thing did not last for more than just a few seconds. There was no fear associated with this, just surprise and what had just happened. And a few questions.

What I believe was that this was the parting shot. I had followed the lifestyle of the evil one and his minions for so long, not that I had ever in my life said, "Hey, I want to go with you," because I would never have done that, but my life and activities certainly lined up with his ways whether I recognized it to or not. Then I made the very conscious decision to make a break and follow Jesus Christ. Overnight, I had made a one-hundred-and-eighty-degree turn and changed my direction completely. This was where I wanted to be, and I was pressing in with full commitment. I was in prayer daily, studying the Word, learning everything I could about my faith walk with Jesus. The other side was not willing to let go so easily. This was their parting shot to say, "Fine, but we are not done." But they were done. I returned to prayer with fervor, realizing what had just taken place, renewed by the commitment to Jesus Christ, and felt very impressed in prayer to start taking away permission from areas in my life that I had previously given to the enemy. I called them out as they came to my mind and said, "No more." Earlier I stated that I strongly believe in the spiritual, and I do. I believe everything has a spiritual component to it. I cannot prove this scripturally, although it can be inferred, but I have often thought that just as we may have guardian angels over us (Matthew 18:10), and where these angels are concerned about the affairs of people and nations, there may also be evil guardians as well, which are fallen angels, who make war with the saints (Revelation 12:7 and Daniel 10:12) who are also out to control areas of your life. I also believe that once you have given the evil side permission to inhabit areas of your life, you need to renounce that permission and take that area back. But that's just me.

What does all of this have to do with the content of this book? Everything.

There is a war going on, and this war has been raging since Lucifer was thrown out of heaven.

This is a war over God's creation, and this war includes you.

It is a war over your mind, your body, your spirit, and your soul. It is a spiritual war to disrupt everything between you and your family, your friends, your co-workers, your church; everything...and quite frankly, between you and yourself, as a means to separate—or to keep you separated from God. It is a war to destroy and kill you.

But God has a plan, and it is a good plan. It is a plan devised before the foundation of the world; we kind of get a glimpse of it in the book of Genesis, further revealed in the Old Testament, and culminated in the New Testament.

God has not left us powerless or at the mercy of the evil one. He has provided a means, a way for us. And He has equipped us with everything we need to succeed. In fact, He has done all of the work. And He has equipped us spiritually. Man, I love this; this is so exciting.

Everything culminates into this: He loves us. And that is what this book is about.

Chapter 3

Let's Go!

    February 17, 1983. This is the day I will remember forever. This was my day. It had been five months since my turnaround, my conscious decision to make a firm commitment to follow and serve Jesus Christ, the creator of heaven and Earth. Five months of repentance, studying, learning, fasting, spiritual warfare, and praying. This was my proving ground. Here is where I learned that commitment is not something that just happens; it is something that you consciously do. It is true in your job, your marriage, and it is true in your spiritual life. And it would be true to say that the past five months had culminated into this day. I had engaged in both spiritual and physical battles yet remained committed. This is not a bragging point on my part, for there is nothing to brag about. It is simply describing the time period I was in.

SALVATION, THE BAPTISM IN THE HOLY SPIRIT, AND THE GIFT OF TONGUES

In these five months, looking back, it is amazing to see the different people God brought into my path. A chance meeting here, an acquaintance there, several people and groups of people come in and out for short periods, all being used by God for me, even if they didn't know it.

One day, I was walking with my tray looking for a seat at Burger King, when I saw an old high school friend named Lori. We were sort of neighbors, sort of friends, sort of acquaintances. We didn't know each other really well, but we knew each other enough to sit and chat. This was not a prompt; this was a divine appointment—because that time with Lori is what changed the spiritual trajectory of everything. I had always thought that Lori was nice, but what I didn't know was that she was a born-again believer—and Spirit-filled. Somehow, as God would have it, and I don't remember how it started, the conversation turned to spiritual matters. We talked for a long time in that Burger King. She saw the journey that I was on and was excited about it because it was one that she had already been through. Lori said she wanted to introduce me to some friends of hers, some that could help me better understand and guide me on the path I was looking for. It was a meeting that I was excited to make. A few days later, early one morning, there is a knock at the door; I answer, and standing there is my sort of neighbor Lori to touch base, see how

I am doing, and let me know that a few of her friends would be getting in touch with me. I had not seen Lori since high school up to that time, and I have not seen Lori since that time, but I have always been grateful for her kindness, graciousness, and obedience because this "chance encounter" (divine appointment) is one of the major things that forever changed my life. She is a spiritual sister that I will see one day on the other side when I can give her a hug and say, "Thank you." I did shortly thereafter meet my new friends, and they were what I would have affectionately called "crazy Christians"—simply sold out to wanting to follow Jesus Christ—in their jobs, their lives, and their associations. They were sold out to following God, and they were kind enough to offer me their friendship and to allow me to join their fellowship. I thought it was cool because they were a group of people from various fellowships and churches all over town. But *this* they had in common, and that was what mattered. This was a really neat season for me to experience this fellowship; it was refreshing from where I had been just a few months before.

Then one night, a few of my new friends took me to a Christian café called The Fishnet. It was just a neat place of food, music, and fellowship. Before walking into the café that night, outside the building, my friends introduced me to a guy named Frenchy. Frenchy was different. Frenchy was for real. He was a little Asian guy, my age or a little older, that was so full of fire—you sensed something different about him right away. He was on another level, and this guy was unreal. He possessed a spiritual authority or power that I had not run into yet. You could sense it. Yep, I was on my path, I had made this sudden and drastic turnaround, and while I was sincere, I was still learning, searching for some things on this new path I was on. But I mean, I was "good," right? I was "in" with these Christian people. I was safe. After all, we can all be better, I thought. Frenchy had a spiritual discernment that was unbelievable, and he layered right through me; this guy was not impressed and wasn't playing—I had never met anybody like him. It was like having a conversation with Saul of Tarsus in the book of Acts on the street called Straight. He was asking me questions, calling me out on things, and everything he said hit me with the hammer of conviction. "You say you are a believer, but you are either serious about this, or you are not," "You can't be halfway or lukewarm." "You are trying to walk this walk in your own power, but you need the power of God. It is all or nothing, or you are just like everybody else being religious." This guy was completely sold out. By this point, I knew of several Christians, but this one was different, he spoke with conviction and spiritual power, and inside, he was where I wanted to be. I literally hung my head and was humbled. I later found out what made him so different.

How committed was I? How serious was I? In my own estimation, I had made a dramatic change, and while that was good, it was not my own estimation that mattered. Talk about a prompt; this night is still, to this day, very important to me. I just stood there outside of the café with my hands in my jacket and my head hanging low, listening and taking in what he was saying. I never saw Frenchy again after that night, although I later learned he had become a missionary, for he was just one of the many people that God was bringing in and out of my life during this season. I knew I was a born-again believer and had been since I was fourteen years old, regardless of the fact that I went off the tracks for a while or, better yet, off the rails. But even in those times, I was God-conscious, just not God-caring or practicing, yet even still, I would never defame God or use His name in vain. Ultimately, I knew to whom I belonged, and I wanted to be back with Him. That's what I had been doing for the past five months, and I knew God was waiting for me. There was more. It was time for a reassessment. Everything I was doing was with a sincere heart, but still, it was in my own power. I was learning, studying, reading a lot, fellowshipping, and listening to tapes and various preachers, but something was missing.

Then, on this particular day—February 17, 1983—like so many other days in this journey, I was driving down

SALVATION, THE BAPTISM IN THE HOLY SPIRIT, AND THE GIFT OF TONGUES

the road, always around noon time, listening to some preachers on the AM radio. This had become my habit. I had found new radio stations and would be in my truck listening to preachers while waiting to go to work in the evening. Going down Kingsley Avenue, I passed this church on my right, and it said Orange Park Assembly of God. My first thought was, *Hey, that's one of those churches, the kind that believes in what I had been searching for.* For the past several months, I had been learning about this thing I had never heard of before called the "baptism in the Holy Spirit." In the past few months, I had read several books about it, timeless classics by the Rev. Dennis Bennett, John Sherrill, Don Bashan, and others, researched everything I could on my own, and read every reference regarding anything about this in the Bible. How could I have missed this? Well, I missed this because not only was this not in my spiritual background growing up, but I soon learned that not all "mainstream" denominations believe in this, and some are downright opposed—even hostile to what I knew to be a very biblical experience. I had learned about some of the churches that were for and the ones that were against. But right now, that did not matter; I knew where I was headed. As I passed the church on my right, I suddenly hit the brakes at the next turn point, made a U-turn in the median, and turned back into the church parking lot. I sat for a few minutes, prayed, and walked through the front door.

I had never been in this church before or ever really noticed it, even though I had driven by it a thousand times, but I was in it now.

I walked in, and there was this very nice lady receptionist; the conversation went something like this:

"Can I help you?"

"Yes, ma'am, I would like to see the pastor."

"Can I tell him what it is about?"

"I would like to be baptized in the Holy Spirit."

She just sort of paused, looked at me, picked up the phone, passed my request to the pastor, and said, "He will be right with you."

I take a seat, and internally, I am anticipating, excited, and nervous.

He walks out, introduces himself, and takes me back to his office.

The preacher goes behind his desk, settles in, and we begin to chat.

The preacher's name was Wendell A. Shaw.

He knows I am not one of his parishioners; that I am literally just someone that just walked in off the street. He asks me about my background and where I go to church ("Nowhere at the moment"), and then he gets to some pertinent questions.

"Are you a born-again Christian?"

"Yes."

"Have you received Jesus Christ as your Lord and Savior?"

"Yes."

"Do you acknowledge that Jesus Christ was God in the flesh who died on the cross for the forgiveness of sin and was raised from the dead?"

"Yes."

Looking back, my thought now is that since he did not know me, he kept asking me the same question in different ways to make sure I was a true born-again believer. Satisfied, we went over a few scriptures, then he then got up from behind his desk, I also stood as Pastor Shaw came around, readjusted back in my chair, and he stood behind me while I sat back down. From there, he laid hands on my head and began to pray, asking Jesus to baptize me in the Holy Spirit. As he was praying, I lifted my arms about halfway and felt the presence of the Holy Spirit flow into my body. The most amazing sensation of peace permeates through me. I was being baptized in the Spirit, and this was real. It is hard to describe, but things were being changed inside. As he was praying for me to be baptized in the Holy Spirit, I was praying and asking to receive when he started to pray in a language that I did not understand. From my reading and studying of the Word, I knew this to be praying in tongues, and it was beautiful. I desired this gift. I wanted this gift. And I knew he was waiting for me to speak in tongues as evidence that I had received the Holy Spirit. But I did have the evidence, and it was internal. If you could imagine yourself one thousand percent completely clean, euphoria would not adequately describe what I was feeling. I sensed—I knew that I had received what I came for.

I do not know if he was disappointed or not, but I did not speak in tongues while sitting in the chair. But man, everything suddenly changed. And I mean everything.

"Anything?" he asked.

"Yes, I did receive," and repeated to him several times that I had received the gift of the Holy Spirit. I felt His presence; He was in my spirit.

I left his office and headed back to my truck, and I am still praying and thanking Jesus. I get in, start the truck up, turn left, head back down Kingsley Ave, and I am still praying and thanking Jesus.

I literally cannot describe this feeling.

I kept repeating over and over, "Thank You, Jesus, my Lord, my God, and my Savior. Thank You, Jesus, my Lord, my God, and my Savior," it must have been a thousand times, just as fast as I could repeat it.

As I am going down the road, I feel this warm churning in my belly. It is like this churning is circling around, literally rolling round and round, and I feel it slowly moving up from my belly, up to my throat, and then out my mouth. In my mind, I am still saying, "Thank You, Jesus, my Lord, my God, and my Savior," when out of my mouth comes this language that I never knew. It was beautiful, and I just let it flow. And the more I let it flow, the quicker it came. Out of my mouth, I was praying in tongues; in my mind, I was saying, "Lord, is this it? Is this it?" and it flowed even more. So out loud, I am praying in tongues; in my mind, I am back to saying over and over again, "Thank You, Jesus, my Lord, my God, and my Savior. Thank You, Jesus, my Lord, my God, my Savior" about a thousand time over, when I suddenly hear this still, small voice say, "That is so you never forget."

This was the most awesome experience in my entire life—spiritual or otherwise. I had received what I had come for, and it was a real-life experience from the book of Acts.

I get home, pull into the driveway, get out of the truck, and see my friend Steve in his driveway across the street. He is just standing there looking at me as I walk over to him; we were the same age, grew up together, and hung out together; we didn't say hi, and neither said a word. I walked up to him, put both of my arms around him and gave him a great big hug, and said, "I love ya, buddy." As I turned and walked back to my house, he said, "What happened to you? What was that about?" I just walked back up the driveway and to the house.

From there, I went to the backyard, near the corner of the house by the A/C unit, knelt down, and prayed both in the Spirit and the understanding for three straight hours. This is no kidding; I had just been baptized in the Holy Spirit and was in the backyard of my house praying and praising and thanking Jesus for three hours. Just before 5 p.m., I got up to get ready to go to work. This ole druggie went to work that night for the first time as a new creation as a Spirit-filled Christian.

On February 17, 1983, twenty-two years old, and since that time, I have endeavored to live a life pleasing to God. The key word here is "endeavored" because by no means have I been a raging success or near perfect, but the intent of my heart since that day has always been the same. I know in whom I believe, and I am confident that He will keep me. My intent since that day, with hits and misses, has been to serve Jesus Christ, the Son of God, God in the flesh, who gave Himself for me—for us.

I believe in salvation through Jesus Christ with every being in my body. I believe in the baptism in the Holy Spirit with every being in my body. And I believe in the true spiritual gifts that God has given us with every being of my body. Yes, I know there are abuses, I know there are charlatans, and I know there are profiteers, but that does not negate the real.

I also know there is the truth. And the truth set me free.

That day when I met Jesus Christ in a new way and the power and presence of the Holy Spirit in Pastor Shaw's office changed my life forever.

SALVATION, THE BAPTISM IN THE HOLY SPIRIT, AND THE GIFT OF TONGUES

As of the date of this writing, that was over thirty-nine years ago.

I would like for you to join me.

Let's go...

Chapter 4

John the Baptist Announces a New Era

I love reading the Bible. I think one of my favorite things is the relation of the Old Testament (old covenant) with the New Testament (new covenant). I also love early Christian writings (The Didache, Eusebius, etc.) and Apostolic Fathers (Polycarp, Papias, Clement, Ignatius, etc.). A lot of what we know about our forebearers in the faith comes from these writings.

I love the history of the Bible and the lives of the ones who went before us in the faith.

And I love Jesus Christ.

I wish I were perfect, but I am not. In fact, I fall woefully short of not even where I want to be but where I should be. Just ask any of my family members.

That is why I have a Savior.

The Jews of antiquity were waiting for a Savior as well. Prophets had prophesized, scribes had written, and the signs had been given. Everything that was written about the Messiah, all of the requirements were out there for one to claim that he was *He*.

It has been said by scholars that there are over seventy major prophecies in the Old Testament relating to the coming Messiah and 270 prophetical ramifications of which each one would have to be fulfilled...exactly—for one to qualify as being the long-awaited Messiah. And consider the fact these prophecies were all in place 450–500 years before Christ was born.

Let me ask you this—what are the chances of someone being born of a virgin (that in itself is a tough requirement to meet)—but not just born of a virgin, but born of a virgin in the town of Bethlehem? Those two right there are pretty staggering odds. These were Old Testament scriptural requirements one had to fulfill to be recognized as the Messiah. But to continue, how that same person being of the lineage of David? Or, even more exact, from the tribe of Judah? Or that He would be taken to Egypt? Or that His ministry would begin in Galilee, speak in parables, perform specific miracles, be celebrated when riding into town on a donkey, then days later to be despised and rejected, betrayed by exactly thirty pieces of silver, pierced in His hands and feet, hung on a cross, no bones broken, for His garments they cast lots, become the perfect sacrifice, abandoned, offered gall and vinegar to quench His thirst, rise from the dead...and the list goes on. All of these actually took place and are prophecies in the Old Testament that would need to be fulfilled by the coming Messiah. Any handful of these fulfillments would be a mathematical improbability, but for one person to fulfill them all is so astronomically inconceivable—it would be impossible. Only one person in the entire course of human history has fulfilled them all.

Jesus Christ.

There is another Old Testament prophecy (Malachi, Isaiah) that has not to do with the Messiah but with someone else, namely His forerunner, known as the one "who was to prepare the way of the Lord" and the "voice of one crying in the wilderness."[1] Not everyone could see the signs or recognize the advent of the coming Messiah, but one did. We know him as John the Baptist.

Matthew chapter 3 starts us off where John the Baptist has been out in the wilderness preaching and baptizing people for some time. He has been telling the people to repent and to make themselves ready because he knows that the Messiah is about to begin His ministry. He is, in fact, actually forewarning them; John wants them to be ready. So he comes right out and tells them (speaking of Jesus): "As for me, I baptize you with water for repentance, but He who is coming after me is mightier than I, and I am not fit to remove His sandals; He will baptize you with the Holy Spirit and fire" (Matthew 3:11, NASB).

What does it mean to be baptized in the Holy Spirit? Well, John was not talking about water baptism because that is what he was doing. John is talking about a different type of baptism, namely a spiritual baptism that the one coming after him came to do. He says to them, "You will be baptized with the Holy Spirit."

We see from these verses two things here. First, there is definitely an experience known as the baptism in the Holy Spirit, and second, the one who does the baptism in the Holy Spirit is Jesus.

The term "baptize you with the Holy Spirit" is not a term that you hear very often today, even though John the Baptist states this is something that Jesus came to do. A couple of reasons for this is because, in some circles of our church, it is said that you are baptized in the Holy Spirit (receive the fullness of the Holy Spirit) when you are saved, or confuse it with water baptism. Other parts of the church say this passed away either when the apostles passed away or when the canon of the New Testament was completed; therefore, this experience was strictly for the early church and is no longer needed. We will talk more about this later, but for now, I wanted you to become familiar with the term baptized in the Holy Spirit.

In John chapter 1, we can see things even more clearly. Here we can see two of the many roles Jesus will have in the life of a believer; one being that He came to take away the sins of the world, and the other as His role as baptizer in the Holy Spirit.

John the Baptist, by now, has acquired the interest of the religious community. He has been preaching a message of repentance, baptizing people in water, and gaining quite a following. The Pharisees (religious leaders) had sent priests and other religious leaders from Jerusalem to find out more about John the Baptist, and due to the crowds he was drawing, they wanted to know if he was claiming to be the Christ (Messiah) who was to come.

The Messiah, meaning the "anointed one," was the one whom the Scriptures foretold God would send to restore His kingdom. The Jews were anxiously awaiting the advent of the Messiah and the restoration of God's kingdom. With John the Baptist creating such a stir out in the wilderness and people flocking from all over from the outlying regions to hear him, the religious community was beginning to wonder if this was he. But again, John tells them that he is not the Christ but that he is preparing the way for Him. Then one day, John sees Jesus coming, and John loudly proclaims to the crowd:

"Behold, the Lamb of God who takes away the sin of the world!" (John 1:29, NASB).

So, John the Baptist has just announced that Jesus is the anointed one, the Messiah who was to restore the kingdom of God. He is the one who has been sent to take away the sins of the world. He is saying that this is the one the Law and the prophets have been attesting to. This is the long-awaited Messiah that they have all been waiting for. But wait, there is more...

> But He [meaning God] who sent me to baptize in water said to me, 'He upon whom you see the Spirit descending and remaining upon Him, this is the one who baptizes in the Holy Spirit.' And I have seen, and have borne witness that this is the Son of God.
> John 1:33 (NASB)

John the Baptist was baptizing in water. He states that there is another type of baptism, the baptism in the Holy Spirit, that, up to that point, was unheard of by most. Did you notice the difference drawn between being baptized in water and being baptized in the Holy Spirit? They have always been two separate events. Keep in mind that this is at the beginning of Jesus' ministry. John's baptism is, in fact, a pre-Christian baptism. To be more exact, it was a Jewish water baptism—a ceremonial washing called a mikveh. John the Baptist, who was the last of the Old Testament prophets, was administering one baptism but proclaiming another baptism that was to come. When he saw Jesus, he knew that time had come.

When we get to the book of Acts, we will again see both baptisms take place; however, by this time, the water baptism is a believer's baptism. People will believe in Jesus Christ, they will be baptized in water, and they will be baptized in the Holy Spirit. The interesting thing is, in the book of Acts, baptizing in water and baptizing in the Holy Spirit do not occur in any particular order, but believing in Jesus Christ always comes first. I bring this up because I wanted you to see there is a distinction made in the Bible between being baptized in water and being baptized in the Holy Spirit because there is sometimes confusion between the two terms when they are, in fact, separate events.

So John the Baptist, in John 1:29, shows that Jesus is the Messiah, the one who was to take away the sins of the world. In verse 33, he says that it is Jesus who will baptize in the Holy Spirit. The question here is, what does it mean to be baptized in the Holy Spirit? Obviously, the term has a meaning. What I would like to do is to show the difference between being born again and being baptized in the Holy Spirit. People will sometimes see the phrase "baptized in the Holy Spirit" in the Bible or a book or hear the term from somebody else without really knowing what it means and would more than likely simply link it with being born again. But there is a difference. Let's look at it.

What It Is to Be Born Again

Let's start out with the words of Jesus in John 3:7 (NASB), where He says, "You must be born again." When we discuss the spiritual experience of being "born again," we must first look at the issue of sin because sin is the whole reason that we need to be born again because sin is what separates us from God. God did not create us with sin; He created us perfect and in His image. Sin is something we, as the human race, decided to bring onto ourselves because we wanted to do things our way, thought we could be good enough on our own, or we are so smart that we don't need God or even need to believe in God. In some cases, we think we can be equal to or be like the one who created us. So it boils down to us just deciding to do things our way instead of His. Sound familiar? It should. We still do it today.

Remember Adam and Eve? God told them that the day they sinned (disobeyed God), they would surely die. And when they sinned, they did die—spiritually first, and later physically. They could have lived forever. Up until the time they sinned, Adam and Eve had perfect fellowship and communion with God both physically and spiritually. After they fell, the spiritual relationship was immediately broken, which is why they tried to "hide" themselves from God. Sin separates man from God. But since the fall of Adam and Eve, God has, throughout time, provided a means to restore the relationship and reconcile mankind back to Him by providing a covering for sin. This act of God is called "atonement," which means that satisfaction for wrongdoing has taken place, and reconciliation between the two parties can be made. Atoning, in short, is when amends have been made for a wrong committed. We do it today with our family and friends all the time. In the case of God's plan of redemption, this "atonement" is wrapped up in something larger called a "covenant." A covenant, simply stated, is a binding agreement between two or more parties. More strictly stated, a covenant is when one party sets the terms that the other party can either accept or reject but not change. In the sense of God's redemption for mankind, when you enter into a covenant with Him, then the atonement, which is already in place, is applied to you.

In this case, the covenant that God established with us is not only a covenant but a blood covenant. Life is the very most sacred thing we have, and life is represented by blood. God provided that covenant for Adam and Eve in Genesis 3:21, where after they sinned, the Lord made them garments of skin and clothed them. Think about this; an animal had to die to shed its blood and give its life to pay for the sins of Adam and Eve. The animal didn't sin; Adam and Eve did. Keep in mind that up to that time, Adam and Eve had probably never seen death. But when God clothed them with the skin of an animal, that means that an innocent victim had died to cover and pay for their sin. This is the first instance where God provided a substitute in our place, which cost the life of something else. Many years later, He would do that again for us on the cross at Calvary when He gave His Son, Jesus Christ, as the innocent substitute on our behalf. Jesus didn't sin; we did. Adam taught the principles of the blood covenant, sacrifice, and substitutionary death to his sons Cain and Abel. Abel, following the covenant with what he was taught, offered the proper blood sacrifice, while Cain did not, offering a different type of sacrifice. The blood sacrifice of Abel was accepted, while the self-made sacrifice of his brother Cain was rejected. Again, doing things our own way...Cain became angry and slew his brother, so we now also have the first murder. But down through the ages, from generation to generation, starting with Adam and Eve, this blood covenant was taught and passed down.

The blood covenant is important because it is the blood that not only represents life; it is life. People in the Old Testament offered these sacrifices as both atonement for sins and thankfulness to God. Noah did this when he got off the ark in Genesis 8:20. Abraham, Isaac, and Jacob all followed with this. Moses on through King David, and all of the people of Israel did as well. This blood covenant was renewed several times and in place from the time of Adam up through the time of Jesus as a covering for sin. However, Jesus said the covenant that He was going to establish would be a new and everlasting covenant, a better covenant, where sins would not be just covered but forgiven. All of the covenants and sacrifices from the time of Adam up to the time of Calvary all pointed to the day when God Himself, in the person of Jesus Christ, would one day be our atonement through His blood. The event of Jesus Christ going to the cross is a blood covenant from God to us.

God says this Himself about the two covenants. Concerning the old covenant, He says in Jeremiah 31:31 (NASB), "'Behold, days are coming,' declares the Lord, 'when I will make a new covenant with the house of Israel and with the house of Judah.'"

So here, God states that at some point in the future, He is going to establish a new covenant with His people and then goes on to say that the day is coming when His Law will not be on tablets of stone (as with Moses), but actually written on people's hearts. When did this day of the new covenant come? Let's listen to Jesus in the book of Luke. Here, Jesus makes a statement that is very interesting. And the statement is this:

Luke 22:20 (NASB), "This cup which is poured out for you is the new covenant in My blood."

Did you catch that? Jesus just established the new covenant.

In the book of Jeremiah, six hundred years before Christ, God says that He was going to bring about a new covenant. The night before His execution, Jesus says, "Here is the new covenant." Jesus is establishing the new and better covenant that God promised way back in Jeremiah. Hebrews 10:9 says He took away the first covenant to establish the second. The day finally came. This scene, taking place in Luke, is what we know as the Last Supper. This is the night of Jesus' betrayal and arrest. This was the night that started His road to Calvary to be crucified. Here, Jesus is telling His disciples that He is going to suffer, pour out His blood for us, and give His body on our behalf. It is interesting that the Last Supper and the crucifixion of Jesus took place at the exact same time during a Jewish feast (holy day) called Passover, which was established by God in the time of Moses and was the day when people sacrificed a lamb and poured out its blood on their behalf to cover their sins. There's that substitutionary death again. That was the exact same thing Jesus did for us. Jesus was—and is—the Lamb.

In Matthew 26:28 (NASB), which is also during the Last Supper, Jesus says, "For this is My blood of the covenant, which is poured out for many for forgiveness of sins."

That is why John the Baptist said, "Behold, the Lamb of God who takes away the sin of the world" (John 1:29, NASB).

The provision from God regarding sin simply stated is this: I love you and want us to have a relationship and fellowship. But your sin is standing in the way, and the penalty for sin is death. The payment for sin must be satisfied, but because I love you, I will provide a substitute to make atonement for your sins.

You see, sin is not free; there is a price to be paid. God spelled this out plainly to Adam and Eve back in the garden. He said, "When you sin, you will surely die."[2] Not only did they die, but it also caused the death of another. Sin is death to us. God spells out the reason for this and how they were to make atonement for sin in the book of Leviticus 17:11 (NASB), "For the life of the flesh is in the blood, and I have given it to you on the altar to make atonement for your souls; for it is the blood by reason of the life that makes atonement."

Hebrews 9:22 (ESV) says this: "Without the shedding of blood there is no forgiveness of sins."

You need to understand these sacrifices were not made because God wanted to kill things or to make anyone suffer; they were designed to show us, we who He created in His image, the seriousness of sin; that sin meant death and separation from Him.

However, He said the day would come when sin would not simply be covered but removed completely. There would be a new covenant that would replace the old covenant. Everything in the old covenant points to the provision made in the new covenant. That day was fulfilled in the person of Jesus Christ when He went to the cross to pay for our sins.

A person is born again when they ask Jesus Christ into their life as their personal Lord and Savior. "Believe in the Lord Jesus, and you shall be saved," Paul and Silas said to the jailer in Acts 16:31 (NASB). We all need a Savior because each of us is separated from God because of sin. When God created us to live in His perfect world (the Garden of Eden), we also had perfect fellowship and relationship with Him. He only asked that we not disobey Him. When we did disobey, that caused our perfect fellowship with God to be broken. That is what sin does. Sin is when we disobey God, and the result of that disobedience is separation from God. But God, because He created us and loves us, did not want our fellowship with Him to remain broken. However, there was something still standing in the way of reconciling us to Him—and that was sin. So God, in His love and His mercy, came to take away the sins of the world. Remember what John the Baptist said concerning Jesus in John 1:29 (NASB)? He said, "Behold, the Lamb of God who takes away the sin of the world." Jesus Himself provided the way and the means by which sin could be forgiven and fellowship restored. Sin is an eternal stain on the human soul. The Bible says in Romans 5:12 that when Adam sinned, that sin was passed down to all generations.

Romans 5:12 (NASB), "Therefore, just as through one man sin entered into the world, and death through sin, and so death spread to all men, because all have sinned."

We are all born into sin because of the original disobedience and transgression of Adam. We are all spiritually dead. That sin, which Adam committed, had eternal implications. Our spirits, which in the beginning had a perfect relationship with God, were now dead to the life of God. Their act of disobedience brought sin into the world and has passed to all since that time. We have all sinned. We have all been disobedient to God. Because of sin, we are all separated from God. The eternal stain of sin, once it was brought into the world, was passed onto us.

The only thing more powerful than the eternal stain is eternal forgiveness.

The only one who can offer eternal forgiveness is God Himself because the sins we commit are sins against Him. So God came to make the provision for eternal forgiveness. God Himself came to us in the form of a man, Jesus Christ, who gave His life on the cross to pay for what we could not, and that was our sins.

In the Old Testament, the lamb, which was offered as a sacrifice for sin, had to be ceremonially perfect, without spot or blemish, to be acceptable to God. That is what Jesus Christ is to us—He is perfect, sinless, without spot or blemish. Jesus Christ was God in the flesh who came into the world and lived a perfect life without sin so He could be the perfect and acceptable sacrifice on our behalf.

John 1:1, 14 (NASB), "In the beginning was the Word, and the Word was with God, and the Word was God ... And the Word became flesh, and dwelt among us."

That is why, through Him, we are accepted by God. We do not have the capacity or the ability to pay for eternal things; only God does. After Jesus died in our place on the cross, He rose from the grave and told His disciples to preach the good news that the way of eternal life was available in His name. When we sincerely ask Jesus Christ into our lives, we confess that we have sinned against Him. It is more than just being sorry for what we have done or how we have lived our lives. We repent (turn away from our ways) and tell God we want to follow His ways. We ask Him to forgive us of our sins—and He does. This is possible because God Himself paid the price for our sins on the cross.

Second Corinthians 5:17–18 (NASB) says this,

> Therefore if any man is in Christ, he is a new creature; the old things passed away; behold, new things have come. Now all these things are from God, who reconciled us to Himself through Christ.

Verse 19 (NASB) continues, "Namely, that God was in Christ reconciling the world to Himself."

That was the whole reason that Jesus was born and went to the cross—it was to pay the penalty of sin for us, and He took the punishment for sin that was due to you and me. With the issue of sin dealt with and the penalty paid for, we can now be reconciled. What does this have to do with being born again? Let me explain a little further:

Jesus Christ took upon Himself every bit of judgment that was rightly due to you and me as a consequence of our disobedience to God. He paid the price that we should have paid. The Bible teaches us in Romans 6:23 that the wages of sin is death. That means that the penalty for transgressing the laws of God is death. What we are talking about here is both physical death (they would now one day physically die) and spiritual death, which means the state of perfect union, relationship, and fellowship with God would be broken. Back in the book of Genesis, the Lord told Adam and Eve they could eat of every tree in the garden but one, and the day they ate from the forbidden tree, they would surely die. When Adam and Eve decided to give into the temptation of satan instead of obeying God, they did die. The moment they disobeyed God (sin), they immediately suffered spiritual death. They were now separated from God, and instead of having that perfect fellowship with

Him, they were spiritually dead and tried to hide from God. It is interesting that satan told them that if they did what he said instead of following God, they would be like God. Then they end up not only trying to hide but also being separated and driven out by the very one they were supposed to be like. Some religions and philosophies today teach that we can be like God or even be a god, but it is the same old lie.

But what Adam and Eve did is the same thing we do today. Don't be too hard on Adam and Eve because we make the same bad choices. If it had not been them that fell, it would have been you or me. Following God is a choice we make daily. In our own way, we try to hide from God. We fail, we cover up, we make excuses, and we hide. And all the while, God just wants us to be reconciled back to Him.

But in His mercy, God has provided a way back to Him. When the human race fell, we were at once separated from God. And because we are sinful, we cannot, of our own accord, work our way back to Him. Remember, we are talking about eternal stain and sin. These are eternal matters which we, as finite beings on this earth, have no ability to fix. So God did. Ephesians 2:8–9 (NASB) puts it this way, "For by grace you have been saved through faith; and that not of yourselves, it is the gift of God; not as a result of works, that no one should boast." That statement right there takes all of our best efforts in earning our place back to God out of the picture. But at the same time, it also takes all of our failings out of the picture. We cannot do it on our own; it is His gift to us, and a gift is not earned but freely given.

This is made possible because of the provision for sin that Jesus made when He went to the cross. We cannot erase, ignore, or cover up our sins and still have fellowship with God, for God, who is holy, cannot have fellowship with sin. Sin cannot reside in the presence of a holy God. Since we cannot make it right on our own, He did it for us.

Consider these biblical truths:

Romans 3:23 (NASB), "For all have sinned and fall short of the glory of God." ("All" means everybody.)

Romans 5:8 (NASB), "While we were yet sinners, Christ died for us." (That is His love.)

John 3:16 (NKJV), "For God so loved the world that He gave His only begotten Son, that whoever believes in Him should not perish but have everlasting life." (This is the way back to God.)

Ephesians 1:7 (NKJV), "In Him we have redemption through His blood, the forgiveness of sins." (This is His provision for the way back to Him because of His love for us.)

Romans 10:9 (NASB),

> That if you confess with your mouth Jesus as Lord, and believe in your heart that God

raised Him from the dead, you shall be saved; for with the heart man believes, resulting in righteousness, and with the mouth he confesses, resulting in salvation.

What this means is this: In the beginning, man had a perfect relationship with God. When man sinned against God, that relationship was broken. The penalty for that was separation from God, which is spiritual death. God is a God of love, but He is also a God of justice. He told us ahead of time there would be a price to pay for transgressing His laws, and that price would have to be paid. Otherwise, justice would not be justice. But just so you know, He is also a God of mercy. He created us and did not want us to be separated from Him forever. Because He loves us, and because He is a God of mercy, He provided the only means for the injustice to be atoned for. We could not do it on our own. Because of sin, we were spiritually dead (Romans 3:23); and something dead cannot bring itself to life. The only one who could do that was God Himself. So while we were still in enmity and separated from God, He Himself provided that atonement for us even though we did not deserve it (Romans 5:8). After all, we chose to sin and disobey God. Why should we deserve His mercy? We do not. But God's love is not human love, and His mercy is not human mercy. Whosoever would be willing to receive this atonement would no longer need to be spiritually dead and separated from God. Forgiveness was now available, sin no longer separates you and God, and God, by the Holy Spirit, can actually dwell in you. The Bible says that if you have received Jesus Christ, you are in the family of God and that the same Spirit that raised Christ from the dead dwells in you (Romans 8:11). You can now be spiritually reborn, which results in eternal life (John 3:16) because you are no longer separated from God. The provision that God made for us not only satisfied the forgiveness of sins but also satisfied the need for justice. Both were perfectly accomplished. In Him, we have redemption because there is a sacrifice for the forgiveness of sin (Ephesians 1:7). To receive that redemption, you confess your need to accept the grace that God has provided for you in Jesus Christ. He will hear you. In doing so, you are crossing a spiritual line from death to life. You acknowledge to Him that you want to turn from your ways (repentance) to His way. You ask Him to come into your heart and forgive you of your sins. When you give your life to Jesus Christ, your sins are forgiven because the provision that He made at the cross is directly applied to you. Justice is satisfied, and grace is provided. You are looked upon as righteous, and the result is salvation (Romans 10:9).

There was a time, in the Old Testament, before the time of Christ, when the high priest would enter the Holy of Holies of the temple and offer a sacrifice (a lamb) to pay for the sins of the people. Jesus is our sacrifice. That is why John the Baptist said, "Behold, the Lamb of God who takes away the sin of the world." John the Baptist understood that Jesus was the Lamb. So when we receive Jesus as our Savior, we are asking Jesus Christ, who went to the cross and paid the penalty for our sins, to forgive us of our sins. It was His blood that paid the penalty for us, so our sins are no longer imputed to us but to the sacrifice that Jesus made. Jesus Christ paid for your sins and mine. Our sins went with Jesus to the cross. Therefore, they are no longer ours, but you need to ask Jesus Christ into your life to receive that forgiveness. Remember that we said that the wages of sin is death? He paid the wages. He provided that death for us, just like God did for Adam and Eve back in the Garden of Eden. Except that when Jesus Christ died in our place, He did not just "cover" sin; He took the actual penalty of sin and the punishment of death for us. Then He rose from the dead. And His promise is that He will raise us also. We see grace and mercy at work, love in action, and justice satisfied.

This is why whenever I look at denominations or other religions, the first thing I always want to know is this: What do they say about the person of Jesus Christ? Who is He to them? What is His nature, how was He born, and what was His purpose here on Earth? Do they even believe in the historical Jesus Christ or believe He even existed? Everything hinges on this. Any group that does not believe or teach that Jesus Christ is God in the flesh, born of a virgin by the power of the Holy Spirit, lived a sinless life in order to give His life as a ransom to us, was crucified, died, and rose again is a false teaching. That is the starting point. Everything else goes from there.

    Several years ago, I was relating this story to a friend of mine. I was using the analogy of standing before a judge for a speeding ticket. In the story, the judge is God, the ticket is sin, and the one standing before the judge is you. You are obviously guilty of speeding, and you are waiting for the judge to pass sentence. My friend is beginning to understand the idea of forgiveness, and he says, "So you mean, it's like I am guilty, and because I tell the judge that I am guilty, he forgives the ticket?" I almost say, "Yes," but then I think for a second, and then I tell him, "No, it's like you are guilty, you tell the judge you are guilty, but you ask for his mercy and forgiveness. However, he can't just forgive the ticket without having the penalty paid because that would not be satisfying justice. So what the judge does is stand up from behind his seat, take his robe off, come down to stand where you are standing, and pay the fine for you. He wants to give you mercy, but the price still has to be paid." This is exactly what Jesus did for us. He came down from heaven, stood where we are, and paid the price for us. God gave us perfect mercy and, at the same time, satisfied perfect justice. He is a good God.

When you receive Christ, your sins are no longer accounted to you. You are clean. Forgiven. The Holy Spirit actually enters you and quickens your once-dead spirit (separated from God) to be alive to God (reborn), and you can now be at peace and fellowship with God because sin is no longer standing in the way.

Titus 3:4–7 (NASB) puts it this way:

> But when the kindness of God our Savior and His love for mankind appeared, He saved us, not on the basis of deeds which we have done in righteousness, but according to His mercy, by the washing of regeneration and renewing by the Holy Spirit, whom He poured out upon us richly through Jesus Christ our Savior, that being justified by His grace we might be made heirs according to the hope of eternal life.

Or, as Colossians 2:13–14 (NASB) so wonderfully puts it:

> He made you alive together with Him, having forgiven us all our transgressions, having canceled out the certificate of debt consisting

of decrees against us and which was hostile to us; and He has taken it out of the way, having nailed it to the cross.

He made you alive together with Him. You were spiritually dead. He has made you alive (reborn spiritually) to be with Him. This is what it means to be "born again." It is a spiritual rebirth wherein your spirit is made alive by the Holy Spirit to have fellowship with God by receiving His Son, Jesus Christ, as your personal Lord and Savior. It is entering into the covenant with God by accepting the atonement that He has provided. No other way will do because the offenses we commit are against God. Even an offense we commit against someone else is an offense against God because they are created in His image.

What Paul is saying in the books of Titus and Colossians is that Jesus Christ will give you eternal life, but it is not on the basis of anything you have done to deserve it. It is on the basis of what He has done. That is awesome. And that is a good thing because if it were left up to us to earn it, none of us would make it. That is what born again means. It is an actual spiritual rebirth that comes about by receiving Jesus Christ into your life and receiving what He has already done for you. We are born into the family of God on the merits of Jesus Christ, not our own—because He paid the price and our own merits just are not good enough. The standard to be "good enough" is perfection. The Bible says in Isaiah 64:6 that our own good works are as filthy rags. The very best we could be, no matter how sincere we were or how hard we tried, would not be good enough. The standard is just too high.

Take, for example, three guys who are really good swimmers who one day decide to swim across the Atlantic Ocean. They jump in at the same time, but before too long, one guy gives out and sinks. Well, the other two are much better swimmers, and they keep going. But not too long after, the second guy gives out, and he sinks also. That leaves only the third swimmer. He keeps going for several more miles. This last guy is a really good swimmer; he is better than the two guys that were next to him; in fact, he may even think he is better than everyone else. He tries harder, has been swimming his whole life, practiced a lot, and competed in events. But eventually, he gives out too. No way was he going to make it across the Atlantic. Why? Because as good as he was, or thought he was, even comparing himself to those around him, the standard to make it across was just too high.

It is the same with us trying to be "good enough" to work our way back to God on our own merit. The standard we use to compare ourselves with is usually other people we know. We think we are as good as so-and-so or no worse than somebody else. The problem with this is that the standard we will be measured by is God, not your neighbor. You would have to be as perfect as God to have eternal life without Jesus Christ. If you have ever committed a sin, even one, then the eternal stain we talked about earlier is upon you also, and that, my friend, ruins your perfection. You already fall short. A lot of us think that we are the third swimmer. We think that if we keep going, we can just make it. I am telling you that you will fall short of the goal.

We could never be "good enough" simply because the standard that we would have to reach is to be 100 percent perfect 100 percent of the time. And we cannot do that; only God can. That is why God did it for us. He was the perfect one. He made the perfect sacrifice. He loves us that much. God has had this plan of redemption in the works way before Genesis chapter 3, even before the foundation of the world; this was always His plan. Do not think that you have to be good enough to come to God or to try harder; just let God. Matthew, one of the earliest followers of Jesus, went from being a tax collector to a disciple to an apostle just from following Jesus.

This is not about sizing yourself up against others; Jesus did not say, "Follow other Christians," He did not say, "Follow your friends;" He said, "Follow Me." I do not want you to think you are not good enough to come to Christ, that you are too good or too bad, or that your life has been a wreck and you are not worthy to seek God. Please don't stumble over something behind you or something in your past because Christianity—following Christ—is not a behavioral improvement program; it is a relationship with the creator of the universe—the one who loves you, the one who created you, and the one who has eternity planned for you. This is between you and Him, and God chooses you to be with Him. This is why He has done everything He has done—to make things ready for you. It is about His mercy and His grace, not your goodness.

Nor do I want you to think that you are too good to come to Christ.

And this is why Jesus said, "You must be born again." You were born once physically into this world, and now you need to be spiritually reborn to the life of God.

Remember this: Grace is when God gives us what we do not deserve.

Mercy is when God doesn't give us what we do deserve.

If you are beginning to see this, that we can't make it on our own, that we have all fallen short of the mark, that we need a Savior, let's pray this prayer together and ask Jesus Christ to come into our hearts.

Lord Jesus, I believe now that You came to do for me what I am not able to do. I confess to You that I fall short and that I have sinned against You. I know that You came to pay for my sins by suffering and dying for me in my place on the cross. I know that You were raised from the dead and that You took the penalty that was due to me upon Yourself. Jesus, I ask that You forgive me of my sins, and I ask that You come into my heart and make me a new, born-again creation. My desire is to serve You and to live for You. I give You my heart, my life, and all that I have for Your kingdom and glory. I ask You to fill me with Your presence. I repent of my sins and ask You to be my Lord, my God, and my Savior. I ask this in Your precious name, amen.

If you sincerely prayed that prayer from your heart and truly meant to give your life to God, God has heard your prayer, and you are a born-again, new creature in Christ. This would be a good time to confess any sins that come to mind, find a good Bible-believing church, make a public profession of faith, and follow your decision to follow Christ in water baptism. In Matthew 10:32 (NASB), Jesus says, "Everyone therefore who shall confess Me before men, I will also confess him before My Father who is in heaven."

About finding a good Bible-believing church: I am not leading you to a particular church or denomination. God will lead you to a church. What I want you to understand is that this is about relationship. It is not about going to church (although that is important), being religious (which will not help anybody), or following a list of dos and don'ts. If you have just prayed to give your life to Jesus Christ, we do not come to Him all perfect. What we do is allow the Holy Spirit to have His perfect work done in us. We allow Him to change us into His image. This is about relationship. This is about a relationship with Almighty God, who created you and loved you to the point that He suffered and died in your place so you could spend eternity with Him. Pray and read your Bible. Now that you have given your life to God, let God be in control. The Bible says His Word will not return void but will accomplish the purpose for which it was sent. Let Him, and He will take care of you.

But He also has more for us...

Chapter 5

Okay, but What about This "Baptism in the Holy Spirit" and "Tongues" Stuff?

To be baptized in the Holy Spirit is a different spiritual experience than being born again. Nor is it the same as being baptized in water. When a person is born again, their spirit, which was dead to the life of God, is reborn by the power of the Holy Spirit. The Holy Spirit then dwells with and in the believer. Each born-again believer has the presence of the Holy Spirit within them. I want to be very clear about that. Being baptized in the Holy Spirit does not make one a Christian; having a personal relationship with Jesus Christ as your Lord and Savior does. However, baptism in the Holy Spirit is a powerful tool God has given the Christian believer if they will seek or ask for it. So let's talk about the baptism in the Holy Spirit, what it's about, and its purpose.

The purpose of the baptism in the Holy Spirit, stated simply, is to endue power to the believer. In talking about the baptism in the Holy Spirit, Jesus said in Acts 1:8 (NASB) that you would "receive power when the Holy Spirit has come upon you." This is not to say that you are not a Christian without baptism or that you cannot live a Christian life, but the purpose of the baptism in the Holy Spirit is to better empower you to do so. Jesus said that when this happened, you would be witnesses. That is not to say that you cannot be a witness without baptism, but this is available, one of his provisions to help you to do so. The Bible teaches that baptism in the Holy Spirit is a separate work of God's grace distinct from salvation and which is available after a person has been born again. There are several examples of this in the Scriptures. One of the best examples of this would be by comparing the events of John 20 with Acts chapters 1 and 2. Please follow along in your Bible on this one. Keep in mind that the time difference between John 20 and Acts 2 covers about fifty or so days. Turn there in your Bible, and let's look at it.

When you read John 20:22 (NASB), Jesus has just claimed victory over the grave. He was crucified and taken to the tomb on Friday, in the grave on Saturday, and rose from the grave on Sunday. It is now Sunday evening, and the risen Lord is among His disciples, showing them His hands and His side. They rejoiced when they saw the Lord. Then Jesus breathed on them and said to them, "Receive the Holy Spirit." Notice the

Scriptures do not say that Jesus baptized them in the Holy Spirit. That has not happened as of yet. That will come later. In fact, after Jesus breathed on them and said for them to receive the Holy Spirit, He later still instructed them to wait to be baptized in the Holy Spirit. But we will get to that in a minute. I would like to point out that the Holy Spirit indwells every believer regardless of our theological or doctrinal stance on baptism in the Holy Spirit. The indwelling of the Holy Spirit in the life of a believer has nothing to do with tongues, not tongues, or whatever. The indwelling of the Holy Spirit has to do with the fact that when a person is born again, the Holy Spirit actually abides within the believer. If you are born again into the family of God, the Holy Spirit dwells in you. And that is that. However, in this verse is when the disciples were born again. At this point, the Holy Spirit has indwelt the first believers as part of the new covenant. If we back up a little earlier, before Jesus went to the cross, in John 16, starting with verse 7, Jesus said that it was to their advantage that He go away; for if He did not, "the Helper shall not come to you; but if I go, I will send Him to you. And He, when He comes, will convict the world concerning sin, and righteousness, and judgment" (NASB). The "Helper" that Jesus was referring to is the Holy Spirit. And then, in the same chapter, verse 13 (NASB),

But when He, the Spirit of truth, comes, He will guide you into all the truth; for He will not speak on His own initiative, but whatever He hears, He will speak; and He will disclose to you what is to come.

Sidebar on the Role of the Holy Spirit

Here are but a few of the roles the Holy Spirit has in the world today. He has roles for the believer and for the non-believer. The Holy Spirit could not come to regenerate and indwell believers as part of the new covenant until Jesus rose from the grave. One of the reasons Jesus went away after the crucifixion, as He told His disciples, was to send the Holy Spirit. In this way, the Holy Spirit would be in the world to convict the world of sin, righteousness, and judgment. Sin, because it is our sin that keeps us separated from God. Righteousness, because our own righteousness is just not going to be able to justify us before a perfect and holy God, so God, in His grace through Jesus Christ, will impart His own righteousness to us. And judgment because the truth is that each of us does have a choice. One day, each of us will stand before the throne of God. "He who believes in Him is not judged; he who does not believe has been judged already, because he has not believed in the name of the only begotten Son of God" (John 3:18, NASB). God will one day judge the world. All of this is to show the people of the world that God has provided a way—His way—His path. The way that would be acceptable to Him is the way that He provided. And that way is through Jesus Christ. Jesus Himself said in John 14:6 (NASB), "I am the way, and the truth, and the life; no one comes to the Father, but through Me." The Holy Spirit will convict the world of its lost state, and He will draw people to Jesus Christ. Then, what can happen is what God wants the most—the reason that He did all of this to begin with. We will no longer be at enmity with God. Our sins are forgiven. We have followed God's plan of salvation. That is the role of the Holy Spirit for the lost. Then, in the role of the believer, the Holy Spirit sanctifies the believer; He guides us into all truth. The Holy Spirit is called the helper and the comforter. These are some of the roles of the Holy Spirit for a born-again believer. He is to guide, help, and comfort. So, in John 20, we read where the disciples received the indwelling of the Holy Spirit. But wait...there is more...

Back to the Baptism in the Holy Spirit

Let's turn to Acts 1. By this point, Jesus has been to the cross, risen from the grave, and remember, in John 20, which was after His resurrection, He breathed on

His disciples and told them to receive the Holy Spirit. They are born again. So that work is done. Let's pick up with Acts 1:4 (NASB),

> And gathering them together, He commanded them not to leave Jerusalem, but to wait for what the Father had promised, "Which," He said, "you heard from Me; for John baptized with water, but you shall be baptized with the Holy Spirit not many days from now."

Now, remember, when Jesus told them this, the disciples were already saved. Jesus had already breathed into them the Holy Spirit. So they had the indwelling of the Holy Spirit, but it did not end there. The risen Lord was telling them He had something more for them. And what might that be? It was to wait for what the Father had promised—to be baptized in the Holy Spirit. Look in Acts 1:8 (NASB), "But you shall receive power when the Holy Spirit has come upon you." Then while they were looking on, Jesus was lifted up and received out of their sight. Jesus made the comment that "you shall receive power when the Holy Spirit has come upon you" after He had already breathed the Holy Spirit into them and after they were already born again. They are two separate and distinct works of grace from God.

The sequence of events from John 20 to Acts 1 goes something like this: Jesus raised from the grave...

breathed into the disciples the Holy Spirit...don't leave Jerusalem...wait for the promise...John baptized with water...you will be baptized in the Holy Spirit not many days from now.

Now, remember, Jesus had already breathed on them to be indwelt with the Holy Spirit back in John 20. They are now saved. They are believers. They are born again. Could there be something more for them with the Holy Spirit? In Acts 1, Jesus is telling them to wait for what was promised by the Father and preached on by John the Baptist; and that is to be baptized in the Holy Spirit. Acts 1:3 states that Jesus appeared to the apostles for forty days after He rose from the grave. It was during this time that Jesus taught them things concerning the kingdom of God and also breathed into them the Holy Spirit. It was also during this time that Jesus told them to wait for the promise of the Holy Spirit. We are now fast approaching the day of Pentecost, recorded in Acts 2, that is, fifty or so days after Christ went to the cross. So in John 20, they received the indwelling of the Holy Spirit. Later in Acts 1, Jesus tells them to wait to be baptized in the Holy Spirit.

So there was more, and He wanted them to wait for more. They didn't have too long to wait.

Acts 2:1–4 (NASB),

> And when the day of Pentecost had come, they were all together in one place. And suddenly

there came from heaven a noise like a violent, rushing wind, and it filled the whole house where they were sitting. And there appeared to them tongues as of fire distributing themselves, and they rested on each one of them. And they were all filled with the Holy Spirit and began to speak with other tongues, as the Spirit was giving them utterance.

So in John 20, the disciples received the indwelling of the Holy Spirit. In Acts 2, they were baptized in the Holy Spirit. This was the promise that Jesus told them to wait for back in Acts 1. And why could it be so important that the risen Lord wanted them to wait for that to happen? He told us back in verse 8 of Acts 1, "To receive power...to be witnesses."

Well, let's see what happened with that. After the day of Pentecost, when they were all filled with the Holy Spirit, Jerusalem was turned upside down. Remember earlier when Jesus said to His disciples to "wait for the promise"...that "you shall receive power...to be witnesses"?

Now Peter, the same Peter who just fifty days earlier had cowered and denied the Lord three times, stands up and has a revival...among the same people that had just voted to crucify Jesus.

In chapter 2, verse 33 of Peter's sermon (book of Acts), he says of Jesus, "Therefore having been exalted to the right hand of God, and having received from the Father the promise of the Holy Spirit, He has poured forth this which you both see and hear" (NASB).

Notice that the outpouring of the Holy Spirit was something that was both seen and heard. That is how people knew something was taking place. Well, the people who had just crucified Jesus, the Bible says, were "pierced to the heart" and asked Peter what they should do. His answer?

Acts 2:38 (NASB),

> And Peter said to them, "Repent, and let each of you be baptized in the name of Jesus Christ for the forgiveness of your sins; and you shall receive the gift of the Holy Spirit. For the promise is for you and your children, and for all who are far off, as many as the Lord our God shall call to Himself."

Who is this promise for? You, your children, all who are far off, as many as the Lord our God shall call. After we are saved, could there be something more? Of course. There was for the disciples. There is for you also. It is to be filled with the Holy Spirit. Read Acts 2:4 (NASB) again. "And they were all filled with the Holy Spirit." Is that different from the work of the Holy Spirit in salvation? Absolutely. Remember the events of John

20 and Acts 1? In John 20, on the night of His resurrection, Jesus breathed on them and said to receive the Holy Spirit. In Acts 1, Jesus said to wait to be baptized in the Holy Spirit. In Acts 2, the promise was fulfilled. It was altogether a different experience than the salvation experience. There was a difference between the two in time (around fifty days), place, and dynamics (visible and audible manifestations from being baptized in the Holy Spirit).

Have You Been to Samaria Lately?

Here is a good story. In Acts 8, Saul (later to be the apostle Paul) is doing his best to persecute the church. And Stephen (the first deacon) died as a result of the persecution. The church is scattered. But they were scattered preaching the Word, and Philip went down to Samaria and began proclaiming Christ to them. People believed in Jesus Christ. They were being baptized in His name. Let's pick up with verse 14:
Acts 8:14–17 (NASB),

> Now when the apostles in Jerusalem heard that Samaria had received the word of God, they sent to them Peter and John, who came down and prayed for them, that they might receive the Holy Spirit. For He had not yet

fallen upon any of them; they had simply been baptized in the name of the Lord Jesus. Then they began laying their hands on them, and they were receiving the Holy Spirit.

The point I would like to make here is that Philip had preached the Word, people had believed, and they had been baptized. They were saved when they believed. Agreed? But they were not done. There was more. Peter and John came down to make sure they got more. Remember, they were already saved, already baptized in the name of the Lord Jesus before Peter and John came down. If there were not something more for them, there would have been no need to come to Samaria. But Peter and John came down to see that they got filled with the Holy Spirit.

Acts 8:15 (NASB), "Who came down and prayed for them, that they might receive the Holy Spirit."

That was different than believing and being saved. In Acts 8, we see both the salvation experience and the Holy Spirit experience, but they happened at different times—and that is because they are different events.

But what about the tongues? Acts 8 does not say that anyone spoke in tongues. Of course, it doesn't say that they didn't either. What it does say is this: A magician named Simon had been following around with Philip. The Bible says that Simon astonished many people with his magic arts. However, after he witnessed the true power of God (as opposed to his magic arts), even he believed in the power of their God because he observed great signs and miracles taking place through Philip. When Peter and John came to Samaria, they were praying that the believers in Samaria would receive the Holy Spirit. Let's pick up with verse 17:

Acts 8:17–19,

> Then they began laying their hands on them, and they were receiving the Holy Spirit. Now when Simon saw that the Spirit was bestowed through the laying on of the apostles' hands, he offered them money, saying, "Give this authority to me as well, so that everyone on whom I lay my hands may receive the Holy Spirit."

What did Simon see? I dunno. I wasn't there. But I do know this...he saw something. He saw something different take place than he did when the people of Samaria got saved. It says so in verse 18. He had been with Philip long enough to see people get saved and be baptized; he saw miracles take place. But whatever he witnessed in verse 18 was enough that he offered Peter and John money so that he could do the same thing. Whatever he witnessed was different in time, place, and dynamics than when he saw the same people get saved. Did they speak in tongues? Maybe. Maybe not. They may have spoken in tongues; they may have prophesied. They may not have—the Bible does not say. It could be any number of things or all of them. God is not limited. But there was something different that took place to the point that he tried to buy his way in. In fact, you should finish reading verses 20–24 for Peter's great response to Simon. It is there that we learn that this (being filled with the Holy Spirit, baptized in the Holy Spirit, receiving the Holy Spirit) is a precious gift of God, just like salvation is. But what I am trying to show you is that there is an experience of and from God that is subsequent to and separate from salvation. Christian churches teach that you receive the Holy Spirit when you are saved, and they are right. If you are truly born again, if you are truly saved, the Holy Spirit dwells within you. Some Christian churches teach there is another measure of the Holy Spirit available in your life after salvation, and they would be right also. It is called being filled with the Holy Spirit, or as Jesus puts it, being baptized in the Holy Spirit. And it is available for you.

Be All You Can Be

A similar example is in Acts 10. Just as a point of reference, it is now somewhere between 35 and 40 A. D.

This is the story of Cornelius, who was a Roman centurion and a Gentile (non-Jewish). But he worshiped the true God. He is told in a vision from God to send for Simon, who is called Peter. And like any good centurion who hears from God, he does what he is told. He sends his people for Peter, and when Peter and the brethren arrive, Peter shares the gospel with his whole household.

And at this point, I would like to digress for a moment about the actions of Cornelius. The way this story unfolds, Cornelius, who lives in Caesarea, has been granted a vision by God with an angel who instructs him to send for Peter, who was in Joppa, which he dutifully does.

Now about this same time, Peter was dealing with visions of his own from God, who was busy giving Peter lessons on His plans for the Gentiles (non-Jews) who would soon be entering the church. Otherwise, Peter, being a Jew, never would have gone into the house of a Gentile. But go, he does. And Cornelius was ready for them. Now the awesome thing about the whole event is (I love this part) in Acts 10:24 (NASB), it says, "Now Cornelius was waiting for them, and had called together his relatives and close friends." That is awesome. Cornelius knew he was going to hear a message from God. And because it was a message from God, he wanted everyone who was important to him to be able to hear that same message. What could be more important than hearing a message from God? So Cornelius decides to have church. He invited everyone who was important to him to come to hear the message...and they showed up. It was important enough to him that he wanted his whole family and close friends together for this event.

Cornelius tells Peter in Acts 10:33 (NASB), "Now then, we are all here present before God to hear all that you have been commanded by the Lord." Eternal things mattered to him. His family and close friends mattered to him. What does that say to us? Doesn't that make you want to invite someone to church? Like a relative or a close friend? Doesn't it make you want to help them hear a message from God? Isn't it that important? Okay, digression is over...

So Peter and the brethren who came with him are in the household of Cornelius. And Peter shares with those in his house the gospel of Jesus Christ. Read Acts 10:34–43 for the first recorded message of salvation given to the Gentiles. We will pick up with Acts 10:43:

Acts 10:43–48 (NASB),

> "Of Him [Jesus] all the prophets bear witness that through His name everyone who believes in Him receives forgiveness of sin." While Peter was still speaking these words, the Holy

Spirit fell upon all those who were listening to the message. And all the circumcised believers [the Jewish believers] who had come with Peter were amazed, because the gift of the Holy Spirit had been poured out upon the Gentiles also. For they were hearing them speaking with tongues and exalting God. Then Peter answered, "Surely no one can refuse the water for these to be baptized who have received the Holy Spirit just as we did, can he?" And he ordered them to be baptized in the name of Jesus Christ.

Here, we have the gentiles who hear and believe the message while it is being presented to them; and while they are hearing, they are filled with the Holy Spirit and start speaking with tongues and exalting God. First, they believed; then, they were filled. In this instance, it is almost simultaneous. But the apostles knew they had been filled with the Holy Spirit because they heard them praising God in tongues, then ordered them to be baptized in water. Now, poor Peter, he has to answer to the brethren in Jerusalem because they took issue with him for going to the house of a Gentile, which was forbidden by Jewish law. So Peter explained everything to them in an orderly sequence. And in Acts 11, Peter says to them:

Acts 11:15–16 (NASB),

> And as I began to speak, the Holy Spirit fell upon them, just as He did on us at the beginning. And I remembered the word of the Lord, how He used to say, 'John baptized with water, but you shall be baptized with the Holy Spirit.'

Peter continues in verse 17 (NASB), "If God therefore gave to them the same gift as He gave to us also *after* believing in the Lord Jesus Christ, who was I that I could stand in God's way?" (emphasis by the author). Did you notice that the same gift was given, and that same gift was given *after* believing? And the reason they knew that was the same gift was because they were speaking in tongues?

Do you see the distinction made between believing and being saved, being baptized in water, and the baptism in the Holy Spirit? They are all separate events.

Peter continues, "Surely no one can refuse the water for these to be baptized who have received the Holy Spirit just as we did" (Acts 10:47, NASB). When Peter says, "Just as we did," he means that the household of Cornelius had the same experience that Peter and company did on the day of Pentecost. Peter said, "The Holy Spirit fell upon them, just as He did upon us at the beginning" (Acts 11:15, NASB). That was how Peter knew they had received the Holy Spirit. Peter even recalls the words of the Lord Jesus, "You shall be baptized with the Holy Spirit." Peter equates the experience he witnessed with Cornelius to being baptized in the Holy Spirit just as he was in the beginning. And he knew that was so because they were speaking in tongues. So it is interesting to note that the Lord brought the first Gentile believers into the body of Christ not only by way of the gospel of salvation but also with the baptism in the Holy Spirit. And the way the apostles knew they were baptized in the Holy Spirit was because they were exalting God in tongues. The same way it happened to Peter in the beginning.

So in the case of Cornelius, first they believed the message of Jesus Christ, then they were filled with the Holy Spirit, and lastly, Peter instructed them to be baptized in waster.

Saul...I Mean, Paul...

By the time we get to Acts 19, it is around 55 A. D., and the church is about twenty-five years old. Saul is the main man in the book of Acts now. Remember Saul? He is the one who was persecuting the church and saw Stephen martyred back in Acts 8. In Acts 9, Saul was on his way to Damascus with letters from the high priest to arrest those who were following this new sect called the Christians. His mission is to destroy this new sect of people who are claiming that Jesus is the Messiah who was crucified, died, yet lives, and that salvation is in His name. He wants to bind them and bring them back to Jerusalem. But an interesting thing happens to Saul. Saul, of course, thinks he is helping God out by arresting these people. He kind of acts like we do many times when we think God needs our help in setting people straight. However, on this particular journey to persecute the church, in Acts 9, while traveling to Damascus to search out and persecute the Christians, Saul has a vision from Jesus and is dramatically converted. His name is eventually changed from Saul to Paul; he was dropped to the ground, everyone around him was wondering what was going on, Paul was without sight for three days, had to be led by his companions to Damascus, and he neither ate nor drank for three days until he got right with God. Now that is a conversion. But now Paul is a believer. In fact, Paul was saved when the Lord appeared to him on the street called Straight, and Paul called Jesus "Lord." Then, the Lord sends a cautious disciple (Paul did not have many friends among the Christians for quite a while at first) named Ananias to help Paul out.

Acts 9:17 (NASB), "Brother Saul, the Lord Jesus, who appeared to you on the road by which you were coming, has sent me so that you may regain your sight, and be filled with the Holy Spirit."

Notice that he is not asking Paul to be saved. He knows Paul is already a believer. Jesus Himself tells Ananias that Paul is not only a believer but also a chosen instrument of His. Ananias calls him "brother." Paul was saved when Jesus appeared to him, and he believed. (Talk about a change in travel plans.) So Paul is saved. He is in the fold. But there is more to be done. Ananias says that the Lord Jesus wants Paul to receive his sight and be filled with the Holy Spirit. So Paul was filled with the Holy Spirit after he was saved. Paul was saved on the road to Damascus. He was filled with the Holy Spirit in the household of Ananias. Notice again that they were different experiences, and the experiences are separated and distinguished by time and place.

There is a spiritual experience available for every believer in Jesus Christ that is separate from and subsequent to salvation. It is called the baptism in the Holy Spirit, and this is something God has made available for you and wants you to have so that you can enter into a deeper dimension of relationship and power with him. This is one of His gifts and something He has made available for you to help you to be able to serve Him better, be stronger, be witnesses, and have power. The Scriptures show this over and over. Jesus taught the disciples about it; they experienced it, believers down through the ages have experienced it, and you can too.

Turn to Acts 19:1–6 (NASB). Such a great story. Paul is now at Ephesus, where he finds some disciples. But Paul knows something here is different—he feels something is missing. So, he asks them, "Did you receive the Holy Spirit when you believed?" (Obviously, there is an option). They said, "No, we have not even heard whether there is a Holy Spirit" (verse 2). Paul then discovers that they were baptized into John's baptism. Paul explains that John the Baptist was baptizing people to believe in the one coming after him, that is, in Jesus. And when he explained this, they believed and were baptized in the name of the Lord Jesus. Now, verse 6:

Acts 19:6 (NASB), "And when Paul laid his hands upon them, the Holy Spirit came on them, and they began speaking with other tongues and prophesying."

So, they believed. That means they were saved.

Then they were baptized in water.

That means after they were saved, they were baptized in water.

After that, when Paul laid hands on them, the Holy Spirit came on them...

That means after they were saved and after they were baptized in water, they were baptized in the Holy Spirit.

Again, the baptism in the Holy Spirit was different in the time, place, and dynamics than their salvation experience.

Earlier, we took a little sidebar about some of the roles of the Holy Spirit for the believer and the non-believer. While the manifestation of the Holy Spirit is different in the New Testament, I do not want you to think that the presence of the Holy Spirit in human affairs is limited to the New Testament. The role, power, and influence of the Holy Spirit are present throughout the Old Testament as well. In Genesis chapter 1, the Holy Spirit is present in creation; in Exodus 31:3, during the time of Moses, the Holy Spirit fills Bezalel, the craftsman, with the knowledge to make fine articles in bronze, silver, and gold. In the book of Numbers, chapter 11, verse 25, the Holy Spirit fills seventy elders who began to prophesy in the camp. A young man ran to Moses about them prophesying in the camp, and our great hero Joshua told Moses to make them stop. What was Moses' reply? He says, "Are you jealous for my sake? Would that all the Lord's people were prophets, that the Lord would put His Spirit upon them!" (Numbers 11:29, NASB). In Psalm 51:11, King David beseeched the Lord not to take His Holy Spirit from him, Isaiah looked toward the future when the Holy Spirit would be poured out from on high, and the prophet Micah said in 3:8 (NASB) that "on the other hand I am filled with power— With the Spirit of the Lord."

And let's look at what the prophet Joel said, also looking to the future, where the promise of the Holy Spirit is given:

Joel 2:28 (NASB),

> And it will come about after this That I will pour out My Spirit on all mankind; And your sons and daughters will prophesy, Your old men will dream dreams, Your young men will see visions. And even on the male and female servants I will pour out my Spirit in those days.

It was this very verse from the Old Testament book of Joel that Peter referenced in Acts chapter 2 on the day of Pentecost when they were all filled with the Holy Spirit.

Chapter 6

Let's Dig a Little Deeper

As we can see, believers being "filled with the Holy Spirit" or "baptized in the Holy Spirit" is something that is supposed to happen to Christians. But Christians have an option to be or not to be. We saw that with Paul at Ephesus, we saw that when Philip went to Samaria, and we see it today. It does not make you any more or less of a Christian; it does not make you more or less saved. It does give you a greater capacity and power to live your life serving God. The Bible says it is to give you power, to be witnesses. I am not saying that you cannot be a witness for Jesus without it, nor am I saying that you do not have spiritual authority or power without it. What I am saying is this: there is a spiritual dynamic that takes place in your life when you receive this gift and blessing from God. This experience has never gone away because, as Acts 2:39 (NASB) puts it, "The promise is for you and your children, and for all who are afar off, as many as the Lord our God shall call to Himself."

But what about the issue of "tongues," and where does that come into play? In every instance, people who were filled with the Holy Spirit either spoke with tongues, praised God in tongues, etc., or you could deduce from the text that they did. Except for Paul. Acts does not mention that Paul spoke with tongues. But as we shall soon see...

So what are tongues? Is it for today? Did it not end when the last apostle died? Or when the Bible was finished? What good is it? Does this have any value? Does it mean anything? Let's talk about tongues. Let's talk about speaking in tongues, praying in tongues, or as Paul and Jude called it, "praying in the Holy Ghost." Remember Paul? He's awesome, isn't he? Since he wrote about two-thirds of the New Testament, he had a lot to say about tongues. He used tongues a lot. In fact, even though the book of Acts does not mention it, Paul himself said in 1 Corinthians that he spoke in tongues more than anybody.

First Corinthians chapters 12–14: We will spend a lot of time here. Everything in chapters 12–14 can be summed up in 14:40 (NASB), and there, Paul says, "But let all things be done properly and in an orderly manner."

That is really the point that Paul is trying to get across to the church at Corinth. Paul never makes an argument for or against tongues or for any of the spiritual gifts for that matter; he takes it for granted that their use will be in operation the way the Lord said they should be. The gifts of the Holy Spirit were given to the body of Christ for a purpose. The only thing Paul wants to see is the gifts used in a proper manner. He starts in chapter 12, explaining the use of spiritual gifts.

First Corinthians 12:1 (NASB), " Now concerning spiritual gifts, brethren, I do not want you to be unaware." The apostle Paul is going to help them sort out their problems and questions. He explains in these verses how the Spirit distributes to each member of the body as the Spirit wills, that there are a variety of gifts but the same Spirit, and that each is given a manifestation for the common good of the body of Christ. And the common good for the body of Christ (12:7) has never gone away or left the church. The church today still needs spiritual gifts to serve God and each other. Since tongues seem to be the biggest stumbling block, we will focus on that, and we will talk about the difference between speaking in tongues and praying in tongues. They are different functions, each for a different purpose.

First Corinthians 13:1 (NASB), "If I speak with tongues of men and of angels."

Paul is talking about two different things here... tongues of men and tongues of angels...two entirely different things. This is where a lot of misunderstanding comes in because people sometimes do not separate the two. Tongues of men would, of course, be an intelligible or understandable language (of which there are over 7,000 known languages in the world), but only if you knew that particular language or God supernaturally gave you an understanding of that language. But it would be tongues of men because it would be a language that is spoken somewhere around the world. The other, tongues of angels, would be a heavenly or spiritual language. Let's talk about tongues and give some examples.

Tongues of men would be when a message is given by someone in a language that is a known language, but the speaker has never learned or studied that language. The speaker has supernaturally been given the ability to speak in that language. An example of this would be that someone could give a message in tongues from one of the dialects or languages that are in existence in the world today. The speaker may not understand where it is from or know what they are saying, but quite possibly, someone in the congregation does. God, in that instance, supernaturally gave them the ability to speak that language. Another example of "tongues of men" would be this: Let's say you are speaking to a group of people from different parts of the world, and each of them only knows their own language. As you speak in your own language, everyone in the crowd understands you in their own language. If you are speaking English, people from China would hear you speaking Chinese, people from Spain would hear Spanish, people from Portugal would hear Portuguese, etc.

This may seem really simplified, but don't laugh because that is exactly what happened in Acts chapter 2.

Acts 2:4–8 (NASB),

> And they were all filled with the Holy Spirit and began to speak with other tongues, as the Spirit was giving them utterance. Now there were Jews living in Jerusalem, devout men, from every nation under heaven. And when this sound occurred, the multitude came together, and were bewildered, because they were each one hearing them speak in his own language. And they were amazed and marveled, saying, "Why, are not all these who are speaking Galileans? And how is it that we each hear them in our own language to which we were born?"

The other, the tongues of angels, would be a heavenly or spiritual language that is not known this side of heaven and can only be understood if God gives the meaning. Keep in mind that Paul mentions both types of languages in 1 Corinthians 13:1, so they both do exist.

This is important to remember because, on the day of Pentecost, in Acts 2, with the 120 people in the upper room, that was tongues of men. Most everybody that heard the disciples understood what they were saying—but they understood them in their own native tongue. So out of the 120 that were speaking in the upper room, either God had them speaking in their own native tongue, and everybody in the crowd understood them in their own native tongue, or, out of the 120 in the upper room, they were all speaking different languages, and those from the different areas understood the ones that were speaking in their own language. We weren't there, so we don't know; we only know what the Bible says, and what the Bible says is that they were speaking in other tongues. It was a miraculous thing, but the point is, the language was understandable—it's just that everybody that heard them speaking understood them in their own language. (Except some assumed they were drunk and probably did not understand anything.) But everyone that did understand what was being said, only in a different language. Still a miracle, but the next point is that tongues are not always understood. I say all this because one of the main stumbling blocks to the issue of tongues is that people fail to see the value of something if they cannot understand it. However, the other side to that is that the Bible teaches us that this is definitely something that God has given to His church. So before we belittle something too much, that last point needs to be kept in mind. It would be better to try to understand something that God has given to us than to just throw it out because we do not understand it. In fact, the 120 in the upper room may not have even known what it was they were saying. That is why the Bible calls it "speaking in an unknown tongue." The point is that they were speaking to people in a human language, and the people understood them. The Bible says that it may be tongues of men or tongues of angels. Either way, it is a supernatural ability language that is from God. But there is another type of tongues. Listen carefully:

First Corinthians 14:2 (NASB), "For one who speaks in a tongue does not speak to men, but to God; for no one understands, but in his spirit he speaks mysteries [secret truths, hidden things]."

Number 1: You are speaking to God, not to man.

Number 2: No one understands.

Number 3: What you are speaking comes from your spirit.

Number 4: You are speaking mysteries.

So there are times when tongues are understood; there are times when they are not. This is one of the big stumbling blocks for people who have trouble with this. They will ask, "What good can it be if I do not understand it?" To which the truthful, obvious answer is, "Why does that even matter?" The important thing is that you are speaking to God in a manner that He gave you to do so. I think we would all agree that it is important to speak to God, especially since the words are coming from the Holy Spirit. And since God is the one who gives it to you, then in that regard, it does not matter if you understand it or not. It is a Holy Spirit prayer given to you by God Himself. This is exactly what happened to me in the truck after I left the church that day when I pulled in off the street to meet with the pastor.

First Corinthians 14:4 (NASB), "One who speaks in a tongue edifies himself."

Now, this is a good thing. To edify means to "build up," and one of the ways to do that is by the gift of tongues. We all need edifying. We should be edifying each other in the church and outside of the church. I have read and heard that some take this to be a negative statement that Paul gives with regard to speaking in tongues—as if to edify yourself is something improper, selfish, or leading one to be "puffed up." That could not be further from the truth. Paul is talking about building up your spiritual man. This has nothing to do with being selfish; it has to do with being a spiritual exercise to build up your inner man, making yourself stronger. If it were meant to be a negative statement, he would never have said in verse 5 (NASB), "Now I wish that you all spoke with tongues." Nothing negative about that. Paul himself spoke in tongues. Nothing negative about that, either. Later on, Paul will say, "Do not forbid to speak in tongues" (1 Corinthians 14:39, NASB). Can't find anything negative in there. The apostle Paul would not have you do something that was a spiritual mistake. To edify yourself spiritually is a good thing. It will build you up and make you stronger to minister and work with people and through situations. If you read verse 4 in context with the beginning and the rest of chapter 14, you will see that edifying yourself is something desirable. Remember, what Paul is doing here is instructing the church at Corinth on the proper and orderly use of the gifts. He never says that any of the gifts of the Holy Spirit are bad or wrong. He simply says to use them properly. People, for some reason, think that because God gives us a gift, we should be perfect in that gift and never mess up. How many times have you fallen since you were saved? Your salvation was a gift. It is a perfect gift. But we are imperfect people. Anytime man gets involved with something from God (whether it be our walk, our church, relationships, etc.), we bring imperfection to something God has given to us. We are a work in progress. That is why we have a Savior who constantly makes intercession for us exactly for that reason—because we are imperfect. The gift of tongues is a means to edify. In the same chapter, he says that prophecy is for the edifying of the church. Both are good. Both should be utilized. God has given both to equip the body.

First Corinthians 14:1–5 (NASB),

> Pursue love, yet desire earnestly spiritual gifts, but especially that you may prophesy. For one who speaks in a tongue does not speak to men, but to God; for no one understands, but in his spirit he speaks mysteries. But one who prophesies speaks to men for edification and exhortation and consolation. One who speaks in a tongue edifies himself; but one who prophesies edifies the church. Now I wish that you all spoke in tongues, but even more that you would prophesy; and greater is one who prophesies than one who speaks in tongues, unless he interprets, so that the church may receive edifying.

In verse 6, Paul explains that there is no benefit to those assembled in the church for one to speak in tongues when there is no understanding. He does not say that for you to speak in tongues is always unprofitable, just not profitable in certain circumstances. In verse 9, he states that it is akin to speaking into the air. There would be no understanding. You would be ministering to nobody. And that is what Paul is trying to avoid.

First Corinthians 14:11–12 (NASB),

If then I do not know the meaning of the language, I shall be to the one who speaks a barbarian, and the one who speaks will be a barbarian to me. So also you, since you are zealous of spiritual gifts, seek to abound for the edification of the church.

Do you see what Paul is trying to avoid? He is trying to correct excesses and misunderstandings. He is trying to bring order. That was the whole reason God had him write this section. The greatest ministry is to the most people in the body of the church. That is why Paul says in verse 13 that one who speaks in a tongue should pray that he interprets because tongues coupled with interpretation would benefit the body.

First Corinthians 14:39–40 (NASB), "Therefore, my brethren, desire earnestly to prophesy, and do not forbid to speak in tongues. But let all things be done properly and in an orderly manner."

Bingo. Paul wants the church to receive edification. Paul wants the individual to receive edification. But Paul does not want the church to suffer for the sake of the individual. He just wants things to be done properly and in order for the benefit of all. But if you use tongues as a private prayer language, you edify yourself. You recharge yourself. You build up your inner man. That is what is meant by "edifies himself." It is a good thing to do, and that is one of the purposes of speaking in tongues.

Look at what Jude says, "But you, beloved, building yourselves up on your most holy faith; praying in the Holy Spirit" (Jude 1:20, NASB).

What kind of faith? Most Holy. What are you doing? Building yourself up. How do you do it? By praying in the Holy Spirit. You are building yourself up. Edifying yourself. The exact same thing Paul said. But what does Paul mean by "praying in the Spirit," or what does Jude mean by "praying in the Holy Spirit"? They are both talking about praying in tongues. Well, is praying in the Spirit (or praying in the Holy Ghost—KJV) the same thing as praying in tongues? Back to Paul...

First Corinthians 14:14–15 (AMP),

> For if I pray in a tongue, my spirit prays {by the Holy Spirit with me}, but my mind is unproductive [because it does not understand what my spirit is praying]. Then what am I to do? I will pray with the spirit [by the Holy Spirit that is within me] and I will pray with the mind [using words I understand]; I will sing with the spirit [by the Holy Spirit that is within me] and I will sing with the mind [using words I understand].

Here we see that praying in the Spirit is the same thing as praying in tongues. (The Greek word used for the word "in" can be translated as "in, with, or by.") Please notice that in verse 14, he starts out specifically talking about praying in tongues. He says, "For if I pray in a tongue." Yet, in verse 15, he calls it "praying with the spirit." Look at it—that is exactly what he says. Praying in tongues is the same as praying in the Spirit.

I pray in a tongue...my spirit prays...shall pray with the Spirit...pray with the understanding also...sing with the Spirit...sing with the understanding. Praying in the Spirit, with the Spirit, or by the Spirit is the same as praying in tongues. Otherwise, if you are not praying in tongues, you are praying with your understanding. Paul says to do both.

Still not convinced? First Corinthians 14:16–17 (NASB),

> Otherwise if you bless in the spirit only, how will the one who fills the place of the ungifted say the "Amen" at your giving of thanks, since he does not know what you are saying? For you are giving thanks well enough, but the other man is not edified.

Paul is talking about tongues, and he calls it "blessing in the spirit." And by the way, he also says that you are "giving thanks well enough."

Back up to 1 Corinthians 14:2 (NASB), "For one who speaks in a tongue does not speak to men, but to God; for no one understands, but in his spirit he speaks mysteries."

Praying in the Spirit is the same as praying in tongues. The other man is not edified because he does not know what you are saying, and that is because he is ungifted in that area because you are speaking in tongues. (You may also speak with tongues yet still be ungifted in the understanding—which is why Paul says to pray that you may interpret.) Remember earlier we said that tongues are not always understood? The last few verses we went over are a perfect example. But that does not make it wrong or bad. Remember, the apostle Paul spoke and prayed in tongues. He even said in 1 Corinthians 14:5 (NASB), "Now I wish that you all spoke in tongues." If there was not any value in it, I hardly think that Paul would have made a statement like that. And he definitely practiced what he preached. Just so you know, this is one of the things people misunderstand about the use of tongues, saying that if you can't understand it, it has no value—totally missing the point of what Paul is trying to say. It is like the church of Corinth in reverse. But there are times it is interpreted. There are times it is understood. And there are times when tongues are used as a powerful prayer language, whether you understand the meaning of the words or not. And what about the good things Paul says about it? What about the benefits of praying in tongues? You know, the part about speaking to God, speaking mysteries, giving thanks, blessing, and edification? Why not do as Paul says and pray with the spirit and with understanding? It is like throwing out the baby with the bath water, then coming back and throwing out the baby tub too. Again, Paul is not saying that speaking in tongues or praying in tongues is wrong; on the contrary, he is simply saying to use the gifts properly and in love (1 Corinthians 13). There can be no doubt that praying in the Spirit is the same as praying in tongues. And this is a gift that God has given the body of Christ for the benefit of the body of Christ.

Chapter 7

So, Where Do We Go From Here?

I spent so much time on the topic of praying in the Spirit and praying in tongues because it is an important point. People will read over those verses in the Bible without really thinking about what they mean. I've often wondered, since the apostles Paul and Jude told us to "pray in the spirit," how do people do that if they do not believe in praying in tongues? I have asked some people and read some things, but none of them line up with what the Scriptures say it is. It usually goes something like, "Well, it's when you are praying really hard" or, "It's when you do not know how to pray, so the Holy Spirit helps you," and then quotes the verse from Romans 8:26. And I would agree that the Holy Spirit is with us in every situation. But that is not the biblical definition of praying in the Spirit. First Corinthians 14:14–15 is the biblical definition of praying in the Spirit.

SALVATION, THE BAPTISM IN THE HOLY SPIRIT, AND THE GIFT OF TONGUES

As a side note, many will use Romans 8:26 as an argument to say that this verse is specifically talking about praying in the Spirit or praying in tongues. I would agree that this could be one of the avenues that this verse is referring to, but to say it is specifically and only talking about praying in tongues is defiantly incorrect. Let me show you why:

Romans 8:26–27 (NASB),

> And in the same way the Spirit also helps our weakness; for we do not know how to pray as we should, but the Spirit Himself intercedes for us with groanings too deep for words; and He who searches the hearts knows what the mind of the Spirit is, because He intercedes for the saints according to the will of God.

What we have here is a great promise from God as to one of the benefits of being a born-again Christian. If you are a born-again believer, this promise is for you. This verse really has to do with the ministry of the Holy Spirit and the avenues He will use to aid and help the believer. And remember, that was one of the reasons Jesus said He had to go away—so the Helper would come. This is a verse that says if you are in fellowship with God through His Son Jesus Christ, then God the Father, God the Son, and God the Holy Spirit are with you and in you, actually interceding for you as only God can, even in your weakest and hardest moments. Or even in your best moments. After all, He is always with you. To take this verse and apply it to anything else would be taking something away that belongs to all born-again believers. This is not a verse that applies only to praying in tongues. It has to do with the fact that the Holy Spirit is always with us. Tongues may be one of the means the Holy Spirit employs here, but it is not the central message of the verse. The central message of this verse is that the Holy Spirit is always here to help His people in every situation. It is a promise, and it is a wonderful verse for all of us. It is a good verse when you are going through a rough time. It is an excellent verse to show the existence and the truth of the trinity. This is not a verse that says, "If you do not pray in tongues, then this verse does not apply to you." This verse applies to all Christians. Of course, if you are not a born-again believer in Jesus Christ, look at this wonderful promise you are missing out on.

My spirit prays. And my spirit prays to God with the help of God. That is really what praying in tongues is all about. Praying to God. The Amplified Bible puts 1 Corinthians 14:15 this way:

> Then what am I to do? I will pray with the spirit [by the Holy Spirit that is within me]

and I will pray with the mind [using words I understand]; I will sing with the spirit [by the Holy Spirit that is within me] and I will sing with the mind [using words I understand].

"My spirit by the Holy Spirit prays" (paraphrased by the author), and in this verse, he is talking about praying in tongues. I shall pray both ways. Pray with the Spirit and with the understanding. And you can sing with the Spirit. The Holy Spirit is awesome. You are edifying yourself, glorifying God, speaking mysteries, and praying about things in a way that you would not otherwise be able to. You are allowing the Holy Spirit to pray through your spirit. Even if the language is unknown, is Paul saying that it is worthless? Of course not. He used tongues himself. Because his mind was unfruitful, did he say not to do it? No way. Why? Because the apostle Paul realized and understood the spiritual significance and the eternal value of speaking and praying in tongues. Is any gift that God gives worthless? Of course not. Should we not desire any gift that God wants to give to His children? And use them? Could He not have done that for a reason? Did God not say that He would take the foolish things of this world to confound the wise? Naturally, the world would not understand this. The problem is that many Christians do not either. Do we always understand why God does things the way He does?

Remember, Paul is teaching to let all things be done properly and in an orderly manner. He is not trying to stop things. He just wants things to be done for the best benefit of the body. That is why in verse 19 of chapter 14, Paul says that in the church, he would rather speak five words with his mind than ten thousand words in a tongue. Why? Because in the church, he wants to be able to instruct others, and he would not be able to do so in tongues. In tongues, he only wants two or three people at the most, and that only if it is interpreted. And if not, then you are to speak silently to yourself and to God. Why? To benefit the body. Verse 26 (NASB) says, "Let all things be done for edification." Everything is meant to benefit, to "build up" the body of Christ as a whole. And part of that includes praying in tongues as a private prayer language.

People are always using the book of 1 Corinthians to show just how messed up the church at Corinth was. Like they were a bad example, and we do not want to be like them. The church in Corinth was not the only church in the known world that utilized spiritual gifts; believers everywhere were using spiritual gifts. The church at Corinth was a blessed and gifted church of the body of Christ. It was a church that was bought with His blood. They had their problems just like we do. We are imperfect people serving a perfect God, and so were they. When people belittle tongues, make fun of it, and talk of how unimportant it is and what little use or value it has, they are actually belittling not only the apostle Paul but also the Lord Jesus Christ Himself. In 1 Corinthians 14:18 (NASB), Paul himself says, "I thank God, I speak in tongues more than you all." If Paul thought it important, I would think that we should too. In verse 19, Paul is putting things in perspective for a church setting. He is not saying that tongues are a bad thing. After all, he just said he spoke in tongues more than anybody. How can it then be bad? Look at 14:39. In verse 39 (NASB), Paul plainly states, "Do not forbid to speak in tongues." Why are churches doing exactly what Paul says not to do? Some churches will kick you out or ask you to leave if you let it be known that you truly believe in this. You do not even have to practice it during the service or in their presence. Your threat to their doctrine and tradition means more to them than your presence in that particular church. I have known several people this has happened to, including myself. And in my case, I was simply visiting the church of a friend. After the service, while chatting with the pastor, he asked what my home church was. When I told him, he said that maybe I should stay there. And that was fine with me. It did not hurt my feelings, but it did embarrass my friend. Not all churches are this way, but some definitely are. And I realize some churches on the other side of the fence are this way too. So again, we have imperfect people working for a perfect God.

I would like to point out that prior to pulling off of the street that day to walk into a church that I had never been to and asked to see the pastor, I had never heard anyone speak in an unknown tongue. Never. During this journey, I didn't bring a lot of baggage in with me. For sure, I had learned that there were some for this and some against this, but I did not have a lot of theological hurdles to overcome. Quite honestly, I didn't know enough to have baggage; it was just simple faith. But I knew God was leading me. I did not speak in tongues while sitting in the chair with that pastor, but I did ten minutes later on the ride home. This brings me to two important points:

You receive the baptism in the Holy Spirit by faith, just like salvation, just like everything else. Everything you receive from God is by faith (Hebrews 11:6), and this is no exception. I was exercising my faith when I pulled into the church parking lot and asked to see the preacher, and I was exercising my faith when I sat in the chair for him to pray over me. And I knew from the witness of the Holy Spirit while sitting in that chair that I had received what I had come for, but I did not speak in an unknown tongue sitting there in the chair. But on the way home, when I felt the Holy Spirit stirring in my belly, I started speaking out by faith. And this language that I had never heard and never learned started to pour out. With no one else there, I started to speak in tongues, and now I know why God did it for me this way for a reason.

You cannot teach someone to speak in tongues. This is a work of God, pure and simple, between God and that person. I am sure that pastor wanted me to speak in tongues while I was sitting in the chair, but he did not force or coerce me, and I am so glad he didn't. He prayed pure, and I received pure. It was totally God. Your goal in your spiritual journey is not about speaking in an unknown tongue; it is about following Jesus and receiving everything He has for you.

Praying in tongues and speaking in tongues have several benefits. If interpreted, it edifies the body. As a private prayer language, it edifies the believer. It is a spiritual prayer from your spirit with the aid of the Holy Spirit, and it is a gift of God. That in and of itself is awesome. How could anybody not want this gift? How could anybody not want a gift—any gift—from God? And you are interceding and praying for things that you would not otherwise have prayed about.

One of the best things a Christian can do is to pray in tongues every day. My drive to work is one of the times I use to pray to God and worship Him. I will use some of that time to pray in tongues. Usually, during worship at church, I will pray in tongues, but not in a way that would be noticed, disturb, or interfere with anybody else. There have been times when I have had this overwhelming impression to pray in tongues "now." When I sense that, I will pray in tongues until I sense that impression release. I did not know why; I just knew that I had to. Praying in tongues is one of the best, one of the most wonderful things that I could recommend for a Christian to do.

I think that people may get a little scared or nervous about things that they do not understand. I think this experience called "the baptism in the Holy Spirit," and the aversion to speaking or praying in tongues is one of them. But this is so powerful. And if people understood that this is a gift from God that He has given to His church (which, in essence, is His body, the body of Christ), some of that would go away. Think of it this way: If God wanted to fill you with His presence to overflowing, would you really care what the result was? Think about it. I mean, since it is God, should we not just say, "Please, Lord, pour it on." Are we close enough to God to be saved but far enough away that we are too self-conscious or care what other people think about how we serve Him?

Could We Use a Little Armor Over Here?

Did you realize that praying in tongues is part of that armor of God that we always hear about in the book of Ephesians? But for some reason, this part seems to always be left off the list when people start quoting the armor of God. Again, I think it is because people do not really know what to do with it—so they gloss over it or leave it out altogether. So let's look at the armor of God. The whole armor.

Ephesians 6:10–14 (NASB),

> Finally, be strong in the Lord and in the strength of His might. Put on the full armor of God, that you may be able to stand firm against the schemes of the devil. For our struggle is not against flesh and blood, but against the rulers, against the powers, against the world forces of this darkness, against the spiritual forces of wickedness in the heavenly places. Therefore, take up the full armor of God that you may be able to resist in the evil day, and having done everything, to stand firm. Stand firm therefore, having:

1. Girded your loins with truth.
2. Put on the breastplate of righteousness.
3. Having shod your feet with the preparation of the gospel of peace.
4. Taking up the shield of faith with which you will be able to extinguish the flaming missiles of the evil one.

5. Take the helmet of salvation.
6. Take the sword of the Spirit, which is the Word of God.
7. With all prayer and petition, pray at all times in the Spirit.
8. Be on the alert with all perseverance and petition for all the saints.

Paul says, "Having done everything," which will help us to stand firm. Well, having done everything, what?

Everything in the list he just gave.

With all (manner and types of) prayer and petition. Pray at all times in the Spirit.

These verses in Ephesians show just how much of a spiritual warfare we really are in on a daily basis. For some reason, when we quote the list of armor, the list usually ends with the "sword of the Spirit." But let me ask you this: Why go into battle missing armor? If praying in the Spirit were not valid for today, why would Paul list it as part of the armor of God? Everything else on the list is valid for today. It would seem to me that Paul is giving the Christians not only a list of essential tools for spiritual warfare but, in essence, a strategy for victorious living over our adversary. The apostle Paul is telling us how to be ready for battle. It would do us well to listen. Please notice that this letter was sent to the church at Ephesus, not to Corinth. It was not only in Corinth that believers prayed in the Spirit; it was the whole church.

Something for You to Think About

Of course, for a person to receive baptism in the Holy Spirit, they must first be born again. Jesus said in Matthew 9:17 that you do not put new wine into old wineskins, but that you put new wine into new wineskins. The wineskin is you; the new wine is the Holy Spirit. You have to be born again (new wineskin) before you receive the infilling of the Holy Spirit. Did you ever stop to think that being "born again" and being "saved" are actually two different things? You are "saved" because you are born again. Being saved is a result of being born again. We, all the time, use the terms interchangeably, and it is no big deal to do so—after all, the one follows the other. But if you are reading this and you are not saved, I want you to consider this: someday, you will come to a place in your heart and realize that you are missing a personal relationship with God. Notice I did not say a personal relationship with religion, church, or denomination. I am talking about a personal relationship with your creator, Almighty God. He has done everything necessary for you to not just know about Him but to actually know Him in a personal way. He Himself took all of the obstacles that we have created out of the way. There will come a time when we all will have to stand before Him. There will come a time when you will have to stand before Him. There will come a time when we will all have to give an account to the one who created us, and with that comes judgment. None of the excuses we use will stand on that day. God wants you to spend eternity with Him, and that is why He took the measures that He did to make it possible. We all need to think about this.

Is Your Relationship with God a River or a Well?

It is a misnomer to think that once we get saved, that is as far as we can go in our relationship with God. Our flesh will constantly battle with us. The adversary is always right there to try to knock us back. Someone who faithfully reads their Bible, spends time in fellowship, spends time in prayer, or any of a number of other spiritual disciplines will obviously have a deeper relationship with God than someone who does none of these things. It is the same way in the natural. The more you spend time with someone, the more you will get to know him or her. And in our relationship with God, we could all do more. Being saved is but the beginning. Being baptized in the Holy Spirit is not the means to an end. No matter where we are in our Christian walk or in our spiritual life, we have not yet attained perfection.

We all know that we could do more, pray more, and live our lives closer to what the Word says. We should make an honest and sincere effort to have as close and as deep a relationship with the Lord Jesus Christ as we possibly can. One of the avenues, which the Lord has given to us, is to receive baptism in the Holy Spirit.

Remember earlier when we said that there was an option on whether you received the baptism in the Holy Spirit or not? I mean, there shouldn't be. There shouldn't even be a question about it. Well, let's follow along in our Bible, where Jesus gives a comparison of spiritual life which is found in John 4:13 and John 7:38.

John 4:13–14 (NASB),

> Jesus answered and said to her, "Everyone who drinks of this water shall thirst again; but whoever drinks of the water that I shall give him shall never thirst; but the water that I shall give him shall become in him a well of water springing up to eternal life."

John 7:38 (NASB),

> He who believes in Me, as the Scripture said, 'From his innermost being shall flow rivers of living water.' But this He spoke of the Spirit, whom those who believed in Him were to re-

ceive; for the Spirit was not yet given, because Jesus was not yet glorified.

Did you catch that? "Whom those who believed in Him were to receive." In John 7:38, Jesus was saying that there would come a time when those who believe in Him would be filled with the presence of the Holy Spirit to the degree that it would be like (in a spiritual sense) a river flowing out of them. That was exactly what happened on the day of Pentecost in Acts 2. First, you believe (born again), and then you receive (the fullness of the Holy Spirit). Just like the way Peter did, just like Paul, like the centurion, like the disciples in Samaria, and just like today. The verse we just looked at in John 7:38 shows the Holy Spirit overflowing in the life of a believer. From his innermost being shall flow rivers of living water. This believer would be baptized or "filled" with the Holy Spirit. Jesus was not talking about receiving eternal life. They would have already had eternal life because they would have been believers. Jesus was talking about believers receiving the fullness of the Holy Spirit.

John 4 is talking about eternal life. Eternal life that comes through believing in Jesus Christ. In other words, salvation. Jesus compares the salvation experience to a well of water springing up to eternal life. And that is good. We want and need to share eternal life through the Lord. That is what we are about. It is part of the great commission. That is what witnessing is all about. In a real sense, you are offering spiritual water from a holy well to the person you are witnessing to.

John 7 is talking about a river, not a well. John 4 is talking about a well. John 4 is talking about someone who needs salvation. John 7 is talking about someone who is a candidate to receive baptism in the Holy Spirit.

When you are born again, you have the well of water that springs up to eternal life. That is the result of being born again. When you are filled with the Holy Spirit, from your innermost being shall flow rivers of living water. That is the result of being baptized in the Holy Spirit. And He specifically said this speaks of the Spirit, whom those who believed in Him were to receive. You see, they would already be believers who already had the presence of the Holy Spirit in them as a result of being born again, yet Jesus said there was more for them to receive in the way of a spiritual blessing. It would go beyond salvation. Remember earlier when we looked at the difference between John 20 and Acts 1? John 20 was when Jesus breathed on them and said to receive the Holy Spirit. That was their well. Acts 1 was when Jesus, after He had already breathed the Holy Spirit into them, told them to tarry in Jerusalem to be baptized in the Holy Spirit. Acts 2 was when the promise of the Father was fulfilled. John 20 was the well. Acts 2 was the river. It is the same thing here.

Do you see the difference? It is the difference between being indwelt and being filled. Between rivers and a well. Both are good. But both are available. So what do you do? Let's look at the book of Luke.

Luke 11:13 (NASB); Jesus is talking here. Here is what He says: "If you then, being evil, know how to give good gifts to your children, how much more shall your heavenly Father give the Holy Spirit to those who ask Him?"

So what do you do? You ask in faith, and let the Lord take care of the rest. Jesus does the work. Remember, it was John the Baptist who said, "This is the one who baptizes in the Holy Spirit." It is Jesus Christ who fills you with the Holy Spirit. You simply need to seek the Lord about this and ask. And ask because you want to serve Him. The Lord Jesus wants to equip you for His service, His body, and His church. He wants to equip you for Him. That is awesome.

Chapter 8

A Little Recap with Some Q and A

What I have attempted to do is to show you from the Word of God that there is an experience, an experience that is rooted in Scripture, which comes from the Lord Jesus Christ, known as the baptism in the Holy Spirit. I wanted this to be in a progressive sequence by starting at the beginning with the proclamation of John the Baptist. John the Baptist did not die under the new covenant; he died under the old covenant. But the baptism in the Holy Spirit actually reaches further back than John the Baptist. The apostle Peter, on the day of Pentecost, says this experience that the people were witnessing is the fulfillment of the Old Testament prophecy spoken of by the prophet Joel. Did you realize that the prophet Isaiah prophetically looked forward to a time when this gift would be available to God's people? How do we know this? The apostle Paul, in talking about speaking with tongues, says so in 1 Corinthians 14:21. The apostle Paul is quoting Isaiah 28:11. Isaiah 28:11 has been a part of God's plan for a long time. So we have a New Testament apostle quoting an Old Testament prophet regarding the gift of tongues.

I then wanted to show you the importance that God places on this experience called baptism in the Holy Spirit. The Lord had John the Baptist proclaim it, and Jesus told His disciples (after He had already breathed the Holy Spirit into them) to wait for it. And then I wanted to show you that there is a difference between being born again and being baptized in the Holy Spirit. This was done by showing several examples of people who were already believers (saved, born again) and yet later received this experience known as the baptism in the Holy Spirit. There is more to a relationship with God than being saved. And there is more to a relationship with God than being baptized in the Holy Spirit. But both are available to whosoever will.

We then talked a little bit about the issue of tongues. I chose tongues because this seems to be one of the main divisive topics among believers today. Some do not understand it; some do not want to understand it. Some abuse it. But that does not make it any less true. I wanted to show you that what the Bible calls "praying in the Spirit" (which we are told in Scripture to do) is the same thing that the Bible calls "speaking in tongues." I wanted to show the difference between speaking in tongues and praying in tongues and the importance and benefits to the believer who will pray in their Holy Spirit-given language. I wanted you to see that praying in the Spirit is part of the armor of God, which the Lord has given to us to aid His children in their spiritual walk. He has not taken this part of the armor away while leaving the rest of the armor on the list. If you look around at society today, we need all of the armor we can get.

And I wanted to express my own lack of understanding when Paul says, "Forbid not to speak in tongues" (1 Corinthians 14:39, paraphrased by the author), why many parts of the church do exactly that.

Okay, But How Do You Answer the Arguments Against This?

Some parts of the church understand what I am talking about, and some do not. I am fully aware that everything written in this book is meaningless if, in fact, you believe all of this has passed away. I would like to look at some of the most common arguments that are used against this view of the baptism in the Holy Spirit and especially speaking in tongues.

These gifts were designed to help the early church get started, and when the Scriptures were completed, the gifts were no longer necessary, so they passed away, according to 1 Corinthians 13:8.

This is perhaps the most often-used argument for the cessation of tongues today. Over the years, I've read it in books, heard preachers preach about it, and heard others say it. If this argument were to fail the test of Scripture, then it almost seems as if over half of the opposition against tongues would also diminish. Let's look at 1 Corinthians 13:8–10 (NASB),

> Love never fails; but if there are gifts of prophecy, they will be done away; if there are tongues, they will cease; if there is knowledge, it will be done away with. For we know in part, and we prophesy in part; but when the perfect comes, the partial will be done away.

Some believe this verse means that tongues have passed away. They believe when Paul says, "But when that which is perfect has come," that Paul is talking about the Bible. Since we have the Bible, and the Bible is the Word of God, we have no need for tongues. I would like to state that Paul cannot possibly mean the Bible in this context for several reasons: Much is made of the fact that the word "perfect" in verse 10 is in the neuter tense in the Greek language, which is the language (Koine Greek) that the entire New Testament was written in. This means that being in the neuter tense, the word "perfect" does not designate a male or female rendering, and therefore it cannot mean a person (actually, a person—Jesus Christ); therefore, it has to mean the Bible since it alone is the perfect Word of God. They say that people who believe in tongues say that we mean this verse is referring to the return of Jesus Christ, and since the word "perfect" is in the neuter sense, that proves that it cannot mean Jesus Christ, and therefore we are wrong, and therefore tongues have passed away. That was a mouth full, wasn't it? Did you follow all of that? Well, the word "perfect" is in the neuter tense, and it is supposed to be because what the apostle Paul is referring to is an event—he is referring to a time when we are face to face with the Lord.

And how do we know this?

Keep reading the very same scripture down to verse 12 (NASB), "For now we see in a mirror dimly, but then face to face."

When? Then. When we are face to face.

Keep reading the rest of verse 12 (NASB), "Now I know in part, but then I shall know fully just as I also have been fully known."

When? Then.

We are only fully known by God Almighty Himself. He knows us better than we know ourselves.

"That which is perfect" refers to a time—an event—a time and a place when we are fully in the presence of the Lord. Then we will see face to face. Then we shall know things fully, and not as in a mirror dimly, and not only knowing in part as we do now. But fully when we are face to face in the presence of the Lord. That is exactly what the context of this passage means, and that is exactly what the apostle Paul is referring to. Otherwise, Paul would have said something like, "You know, when the Scriptures are finished, or when the Bible is finally complete, all of this will go away." But that is not what he said. He said when we are face to face. Now, whether that happens at the rapture, when you die, or at the second coming of Jesus Christ is totally irrelevant. What is relevant is that at that point, you will be with the Lord, you will be face to face, you will know fully just as you have been fully known, and as Paul said, this will pass away. We will not need it.

The apostle Paul fully expected the gifts to be with us until the end of the church age, when we would all be with Christ. He said so himself. First Corinthians 1:5–7 (NASB),

> That in everything you were enriched in Him, in all speech and all knowledge, even as the testimony concerning Christ was confirmed in you, so that you are not lacking in any gift,

awaiting eagerly the revelation of our Lord Jesus Christ.

They were not lacking any gift and were waiting for the return of the Lord. The gifts (all of them) would be with the church at the time of the return of the Lord.

The list of spiritual gifts given by the apostle Paul in 1 Corinthians 12, starting with verse 4 through verse 11 (NASB), is as follows:

> Now there are varieties of gifts, but the same Spirit. And there are varieties of ministries, and the same Lord. And there are varieties of effects, but the same God who works all things in all persons. But to each one is given the manifestation of the Spirit for the common good. For to one is given:

- "The word of wisdom through the Spirit."
- "To another the word of knowledge according to the same Spirit."
- "To another faith by the same Spirit."
- "To another gifts of healing by the one Spirit."
- "And to another the effecting of miracles."
- "And to another prophecy."
- "And to another the distinguishing of spirits."
- "To another various kinds of tongues."
- "And to another the interpretation of tongues."

"But one and the same Spirit works all these things, distributing to each one individually just as He wills."

Romans 12:6–8 lists other gifts given to the church: Paul says, "And since we have gifts that differ according to the grace given to us, let each exercise them accordingly" (Romans 12:6, NASB), then he lists the gifts of prophecy, serving, teaching, exhortation, giving, leadership, mercy.

First Corinthians 12:28–30 lists still more offices in the church He has appointed and gifts given to the church, for the common good, all by the same Spirit, the same Lord, and the same God who works all things in all persons: apostle, prophet, teacher, miracles, kinds of healings, helps, administration, tongues.

The apostle Paul was not alone in his regard for spiritual gifts. Even the apostle Peter chimed in with regard to spiritual gifts, not by giving a list but by encouraging the church to use the gifts to serve each other, to be good stewards of what God has given, and to build up the body of Christ.

First Peter 4:10–11 (NASB) starts out this way:

> As each one has received a special gift, employ it in serving one another, as good stewards of the manifold grace of God. Whoever speaks, let him speak, as it were, the utterances of God; whoever serves, let him do so as by the

strength which God supplies; so that in all things God may be glorified through Jesus Christ.

Have all of these gifts ceased, or do we pick and choose? Paul did not want the church to lack any gift and expected the church to utilize these gifts, which the Lord has given His church until that time when we would be with the Lord.

Back to 1 Corinthians 13 verse 8, Paul says tongues will cease (which we will not need when we are with the Lord), but it also says that knowledge will be done away with, so by that same verse, knowledge must also be gone, because it left with the tongues. And, of course, that is silly. The prophet Daniel himself, in talking about the end times (time of the end), said in Daniel 12:4 that knowledge should increase. Unless, of course, Paul is talking about the spiritual gift of the Word of knowledge which is a gift that is mentioned in 1 Corinthians 12:8 (along with a host of others) and would make sense from the context of the passage. After all, 13:8 (NASB) says, "If there are gifts of prophecy" (a spiritual gift), "If there are tongues" (another spiritual gift), then it would follow that when he says, "If there is knowledge," that would be a spiritual gift also. The truth of the matter is, is that it does not matter what kind of knowledge Paul is talking about. If he is talking about the natural "human" knowledge, that just would not make sense because knowledge is increasing every day. If Paul is talking about the spiritual gift of the Word of knowledge, it still falls in the same category as the "that which is perfect" statement mentioned earlier. Also, if the list of gifts from which the gift of knowledge comes in 1 Corinthians 12:8–10 has passed away, then all of those gifts from that chapter have passed away—including faith. And I would submit to you that is not the case. None of the gifts have passed away. We may have discarded them as a church, ignored them, used them incorrectly, marketed them for profit, and even faked the use of some or all of them, but that does not mean the gifts have left the church. It means that we, as a church, have left gifts. Just because gifts have been misused, that does not negate the true gift.

When we are face to face with the Lord Jesus Christ, everything will all be unexplainably different. Our bodies and everything will be different because when that time comes, we will be living in the spiritual realm. We cannot even begin to fathom what an eternal spiritual existence will be like. All we know is that we will be with the Lord. And that is enough. If you read the whole section of 1 Corinthians 13:8–12, you will see that Paul is talking about a time when we will be with the Lord. "That which is perfect" is that time. Even though the Bible is the perfect Word of God, we are not perfect. Then we shall be. The Bible does not scripturally fit the context of what the apostle Paul is talking about when he says, "That which is perfect." Only being with the Lord does.

Consider this: All of the books of the New Testament were written in a time span of approximately fifty or so years. The last book to be written was Revelation, written sometime in the 90s A. D. During those fifty years, the apostle Paul wrote letters, as did Peter and James; four Gospels were written, Jude wrote a letter, and John, in addition to his Gospel, also wrote a few letters. But not everybody had the same Gospels, the same epistles, or even agreed as to which letters should be included as authoritative. Some areas had some letters, while other areas had others. This was because cities were spread over such a large geographical area, and it took a long time to travel from, say, Corinth to Ephesus. The letters and Gospels were hand-scribed and hand-carried between the different cities. Some cities had letters that they considered authoritative, while others who knew about those letters did not.

Ever heard of the *Epistle of Clement*? Clement was a bishop in the church of Rome and wrote a letter to the church of Corinth around 95 A. D. In the letter, he mentions the "blessed Peter and Paul." He knew both apostles, and tradition has it that they placed him in charge of the church in Rome. Well, the church in Corinth considered it an authoritative letter, treated it as Scripture, and read it in their churches. How about the *Shepherd of Hermas* or *The Didache*? *The Didache* was written around 120 A. D. and was even treated as Scripture in some places. These were all very important writings highly regarded by early Christians. They are still highly regarded today. They give us a glimpse into what life was like for first and second-century Christians. Today, these, along with other early writings, we call Apostolic Fathers because they are the earliest writings we have of prominent Christians who came next in line after the apostles.

Now in an altogether different class, there were also spurious letters and forgeries to contend with. These had to be weeded out. The heretic Marcion in the second century had his own following and wrote his own version of the Gospels. Also, the list of accepted Scripture was not always the same between the church in the East and the West. Some regarded some books as authoritative, while others did not. The book of Jude was one of these contested because of a reference to the Book of Enoch and the apocryphal Assumption of Moses. Early on, there was doubt as to the authenticity of the book of Second Peter. There was a general acceptance of most of the books that today make up our New Testament, but some churches in some areas contested even some of these. It was not as if one day somebody stood up and said, "Hey, here's the Bible...it is finally finished!"

Time and distance was the biggest factor. The church in Rome may have heard there was a letter from Paul over in the Galatia region, but that does not mean they had a copy of it. It took time to compile and agree upon which letters were authoritative—to be considered Scripture—and which were not. This finally happened in 397 A. D. at the Council of Carthage when the East and West got together to ratify what we now know as the twenty-seven books of the New Testament. Just a little church history here, but if tongues passed away when the Bible was completed, was it in the late 90s when Revelation was written, or in the 100s when the Gospels, letters, and epistles were still being collected by various churches, or the 200s when church leaders were trying to decide what was and was not genuine Scripture? Or was it 397 A. D. when everyone finally agreed as to what was what? The completion of the canon of Scripture, regardless of what we consider the timetable, did not do away with any of the spiritual gifts.

Tongues were manifested in Acts chapter 2, so the apostles could go preach throughout the world in languages they did not know.

Oh, I love this. Not only have I repeatedly heard this over the years, but this is what I was taught early on when I became a Christian. The problem is, it just isn't true either scripturally or historically as a singular argument for the use of tongues. The argument is that God empowered the first-century apostles with the ability to speak in languages called "various kinds of tongues" to enable them to spread the gospel to the world. This was the kickoff. First of all, it was not just the apostles who received the baptism in the Holy Spirit with the gift of tongues in Acts chapter 2; there were at least 120 in the upper room on the day of Pentecost, and most of these were not the famous people of the Bible, they were normal believers in Christ, men and women just like you and me. We have gone over several instances where, when the Holy Spirit was poured out, believers spoke in tongues (cf. Acts chapters 2, 8, 10, 19). But there is not one instance in the book of Acts where any of the apostles, believers, or anybody went to preach in tongues to a people in a language they did not know. Not one. Acts chapter 2 recounts when on the day of Pentecost, when they were all filled with the Holy Spirit how everyone heard them speaking heard them in their own language, which is valid and one of the possible benefits of speaking in tongues, but there is not one case or example of, say, Paul, or Peter, or Barnabas going somewhere and speaking in an earthly language that was unknown to them. Also, if this argument were to be valid, Paul would have absolutely mentioned this in his long spiritual gifts section in 1 Corinthians, where he was correcting the Corinthian church in its use of spiritual gifts. Which, of course, he did not, because this was not the singular purpose of this gift as the argument says it is. Paul explicitly states that there are different kinds of tongues; they are not all earthly or human language but also of a spiritual nature. On the day of Pentecost, there was no "interpreter," the people there spoke as the Spirit gave them utterance, and the people heard as the Holy Spirit gave them understanding.

I was taught that the gifts passed away when the apostles passed away.

Paul never taught that the gifts would pass away when the last apostle passed away. In fact, Paul was teaching the church the proper way and order to use the gifts (something we need more of today) so that the body would be built up and edified, so believers would be ministered to and non-believers convicted. He never said, "When we are gone, the gifts are gone." What he did say was that these are gifts God has given to minister to the body, to edify and strengthen the individual and equip the church as a whole. And he wanted the gifts to be used properly for the benefit of the body of Christ. That is why in 1 Corinthians 12:7 (NASB), Paul said, "But to each is given the manifestation of the Spirit for the common good." That is why he lists it as part of the armor of God in the book of Ephesians. The apostle Paul expected the gifts to be in effect until the return of the Lord Jesus, as he outlined in 1 Corinthians 1:5–7 (NASB),

That in everything you were enriched in Him, in all speech and all knowledge, even as the testimony concerning Christ was confirmed in you, so that you are not lacking in any gift, awaiting eagerly the revelation of our Lord Jesus Christ.

He is far from saying the gifts will leave the church; on the contrary, Paul is helping to establish the church through the use of the gifts.

Isn't it true that according to Revelation 22:18–19, this, in essence, would be adding to the Bible?
Revelation 22:18–19 (NASB),

I testify to everyone who hears the words of the prophecy of this book: if anyone adds to them, God shall add to him the plagues which are written in this book; and if anyone takes away from the words of the book of this prophecy, God shall take away his part from the tree of life and from the holy city, which are written in this book.

Revelation 22:18–19 refers to the prophecies that the apostle John saw while on the Isle of Patmos around 90

A. D. John is referring specifically to the book, which became known as the book of Revelation. The entire book of Revelation is a book of prophecy where Jesus Christ gives the apostle John insights, visions, and revelations regarding future events. In Revelation 1:1, John himself writes that he was given visions of things that will shortly take place. He is not referring to the Bible as a whole; he is referring specifically to the prophecies of this book (the book of Revelation) in which he recorded his visions. That is why he says in Revelation 22:18, "I testify to everyone who hears the words of the prophecy of this book." "This book" that he is talking about is the book of Revelation, not what we today call the entire New Testament.

While the Gospels and epistles had been around for thirty to forty years, the Bible, with the collections of books as we know it, did not exist for another 300 years. John himself probably had not read all of the books, letters, and epistles that make up our New Testament.

The gifts do not add to Scripture nor replace the Word of God. The gifts do not add to or replace Scripture, regardless if we are talking about the Old Testament or the New Testament. The canon of Scripture is closed. In fact, Paul mentions in 1 Corinthians 14:29 that everything is to be judged. No prophecy or utterance will ever replace Scripture; it is to be judged by Scripture.

Do not the Scriptures say that not all will speak with tongues?

Yes.

But the apostle Paul makes a distinction between tongues for public ministry and tongues for the individual as a private prayer language. The private prayer language is available for everyone who desires to be baptized in the Holy Spirit.

Let's turn to 1 Corinthians 12 that is referring to the verse in question.

Paul is explaining how the Holy Spirit distributes to each person the gifts as the Spirit wills. He mentions a variety of gifts, a variety of ministries, and a variety of effects. All of these are manifestations of the Spirit (verse 7), and each category of these manifestations is given for the common good (meaning the common good for the body of Christ—also verse 7). Part of the manifestations for the common good is what the Bible calls various kinds of tongues. There is more than one type or manifestation of tongues. (Remember the tongues of men and tongues of angels that Paul spoke about earlier? Also, remember there were times tongues were understood and times they were not. These would be the various kinds of tongues the Bible talks about.) Not everyone will speak in tongues, prophesy, or interpret. Some will operate in some gifts, some in another. Paul is talking about gifts that the Holy Spirit distributes for people to use to minister to the body. When Paul says in 1 Corinthians 12:30 (NASB), "All do not speak with tongues, do they?" he is referring to the public ministry of speaking in tongues, which is meant to be interpreted in the church. That is different from praying in tongues that Paul talks about in 1 Corinthians 14:2. One is a public ministry, the other a private prayer language. The private prayer language is meant for just that—a private prayer language, like in the book of Jude, where he says, "But you, beloved, building yourselves up on your most holy faith; praying in the Holy Spirit" (Jude 1:20, NASB). That would be praying in tongues. You can call it praying in tongues, speaking in tongues, or you can call it one of the different forms of speaking in tongues, but the point is this is altogether different than the public ministry of speaking in tongues. Remember when Paul said, "For one who speaks in a tongue does not speak to men, but to God; for no one understands, but in his spirit he speaks mysteries" (1 Corinthians 14:2, NASB). This is praying in tongues—a private prayer language. In this instance, you are not speaking to men but to God. It is not intended for public ministry. It is intended as a prayer language for you to speak to God.

The public ministry is mentioned in 1 Corinthians 14:27–28 (NASB), where Paul states, "If anyone speaks in a tongue, it should be by two or at the most three, and each in turn, and let one interpret; but if there is no interpreter, let him keep silent in the church."

See the difference? Paul says, "In the church." This is an obvious example of the public ministry of speaking in tongues. You would be speaking to the church, where someone would interpret the message for the body. In one example, you are speaking publicly to the body; in the other, you are speaking only to God—or, as the Amplified Bible says, it is God speaking through your spirit by the Holy Spirit. Why does God do it this way? I don't know...but He does. And it is an awesome thing to be a part of.

So do all speak with tongues? No. All will not possess the ministerial gift of publicly speaking in tongues. But the baptism in the Holy Spirit is received today in the same way as on the day of Pentecost, or with Cornelius, or with the Samaritans, or with any of the other examples in the book of Acts...when they were all filled with the Holy Ghost and spoke with other tongues. Based on scriptural precedent, in every account of the reception of the baptism in the Holy Spirit recorded in the book of Acts, the initial evidence of that experience was or is unmistakably inferred to be that of speaking in other tongues. So yes, you will receive the baptism in the Holy Spirit with the evidence of speaking in other tongues.

Are not tongues the least of the gifts?
Some people belittle tongues (whether they believe in it or not), calling it the "least" of the gifts, and they

do not want to be associated with the least of the gifts or, because it is the least of the gifts, it is not an important gift. Of course, they still reject what would be considered the "greater" gifts, such as prophecy, miracles, healing, etc. It is sad people refuse what they consider the least of the gifts when they will not even accept what they would consider to be the greater gifts. Take, for example, a large church of 5,000 people whose doctrine is opposed to what this book is about. That is what I would call a community of believers. But they do not want anyone who believes in speaking or praying with tongues in their church and will tell you that even if there were such a thing as tongues around today, it is the least of the gifts anyway, so it is no big deal. But they are not even open to what they say the Bible calls the greater gifts. Okay, for example, do all of them in that church speaks with tongues? No. Do all work miracles? No. Do all have the gift of healing? No. (I am paraphrasing 1 Corinthians 12:29–30—if you turn to it, you will see what I am talking about.) Out of 5,000 people, shouldn't somebody have at least one of these greater gifts, even if they don't want the "lesser" gifts? If their church was open to it, they would. But they will tell you that the greatest of the gifts is love, so they will take that one instead. The problem is that people so rarely (if ever) walk in that kind of love. The love they are referring to is in 1 Corinthians 13, which is smack dab in the middle of the spiritual gifts section of 1 Corinthians (chapters 12–14) that we have been talking about. If you read chapter 13, you will see how far short we all fall in what God's idea of love is. And by the way, nowhere is love called a gift. So you can't say, "I'll take the gift of love instead of the gift of tongues." In fact, 1 Corinthians 14 starts out with, "Pursue love, yet earnestly desire spiritual gifts." So I guess what we should do is: pursue love and earnestly desire spiritual gifts.

The first fruit of the Spirit is love. When you are immersed in the Word of God, and your heart is saturated with the Spirit of God, you will be loving. We need to pursue love because we haven't quite made it there yet; not the biblical kind of love, anyway. So we can't say that we reject all of the spiritual gifts because we have the love part instead. Paul says to go for both. And he belittles none of them. Why would anybody want to classify a gift from God (any gift) in such a manner? The apostle Paul did not think of it in such a way.

What if my church is against this?
One of the hardest things to overcome is church tradition. Some churches, no matter what happened, would not accept the doctrine of the baptism in the Holy Spirit, especially the tongues. For some reason, the issue is always on the "tongues." Most everything else can be accepted, such as miracles, healings, or whatever

else, because it falls under the providence of God. And if God wants to heal somebody, He is God, so He can do it. If God wants to perform some other miracle, well, by golly, He is God, so He can do it. But if God wants to fill you with the Holy Ghost with the evidence of speaking in tongues, well, that is altogether a different matter. Church tradition is the same thing Jesus was up against in His earthly ministry. We would do well to listen to what Jesus said about tradition:

Matthew 15:6 (NASB), "And thus you invalidate the word of God for the sake of your tradition."

That is exactly what we do today. All churches do this to some degree. We do not give the Holy Spirit free reign or allow Him to move fully during the service. We have to stick to our schedule and think the service should go this way or that way; we sing our songs, take the offering, do the sermon, sing some more songs, and then go home. We do not want to deviate from the order that we have set up. After all, we should have "order," should we not? But I sometimes feel that our "order" is not always God's "order." Tradition is not a bad thing until we allow it to prevent God from moving among His people. That should strike our hearts, whether it is this topic or any other topic, which keeps us from any blessing from God.

People who believe in this seem to place more emphasis on experience than on Scripture. You should base your beliefs and walk on Scripture.

We do. Do you realize that your salvation experience was an experience based on Scripture? Remember when you first received Jesus Christ as your Lord and Savior? That was a spiritual experience. It is no different with the baptism in the Holy Spirit. Baptism in the Holy Spirit is a spiritual experience that is based on the Word of God. I am sure that after you were saved, you became more aware of God moving in your life and in other people's lives. That is a spiritual experience. Anytime God does something or moves in someone's life would be a spiritual experience. It is not that we as Christians base things on experience rather than Scripture, but experience that lines up with Scripture is awesome. Baptism in the Holy Spirit is a spiritual experience that lines up with Scripture, just as salvation is.

But wait, there is more...

Chapter 9

The Preeminence of Jesus Christ and the Bible

With all of this talk about tongues, spiritual gifts, or any other topic of a particular Christian interest, it is quite easy to get lost in the main thing—or the main person—and that is the person of Jesus Christ.

I am passionate about what this book is about; I believe in this with all of my heart. But I am more passionate about Jesus Christ.

Jesus Christ is God in the flesh; He is both the Lamb of God and the creator of the universe, born of a virgin, who lived a sinless life to be the propitiation for our sins, suffered at the hands and whips of His religious and civil authorities, condemned to death, was nailed to a cross, died, and then rose from the dead. All this was all prophesied millennia beforehand.

That is who Jesus Christ is.

And He did all of this just so that those who believe in Him could be spiritually recreated, to have fellowship and union with God the Father through Him, to be "born again" to receive eternal life. You have sin, sin separates us from God, but Jesus Christ, God in the flesh, paid for those sins. Ask in His name, and He will forgive your sins. Believe in Him. That's it. He will meet you where you are regardless of where you have been or what you have done.

I realize there are many religions of the world out there, religions that come in all shapes and sizes. But at the end of the day, they eventually all boil down to the same ingredient: "works-based" salvation. You have to work for your salvation, eternal life, or whatever is the end result of their belief. Be good enough, and you can come back as something better; be better than your neighbor, and the scales tip in your favor; try hard enough, be religious enough, or sacrifice enough, and you will be rewarded. Every other religion not connected to the person of Jesus Christ has this component of works to their concept of eternal bliss.

But not Christianity. Historic Christianity is the only religion on the face of the planet that says, "It is not about what you have done; it is about what God has done." It is not about works, "For by grace you have been saved through faith; and that is not of yourselves, it is the gift of God; not a result of works, that no one should boast" (Ephesians 2:8–9, NASB). Saved by grace, through faith, not of works, not your own doing, God did it for you, so you can't go around saying how good you are or how you earned it. It was the grace of God and the love of God doing it all for you. That is Christianity with Jesus Christ at its core.

Pontius Pilate once asked Jesus, "What is truth?" Think of this—Pilate, who is standing in front of Jesus Christ, God in the flesh, asks the creator of the universe what truth is. In actuality, the "truth" is standing right before him. "The truth" is His Word, the Holy Scriptures, which is God talking to us. This is exactly what John 1:1–14 says (my paraphrase), "In the beginning was the Word, and the Word was with God, and the Word was God...and the Word became flesh and dwelt among us." Let that sink in: The Word became flesh...the Word that became flesh and dwelt among us was Jesus Christ. Please remember that salvation is not a prayer; although we should pray, it is not a church, although to go to church is a good thing, nor is it a doctrine, philosophy, or theological dissertation. Salvation is a person. And that person is Jesus Christ. He is the Word that became flesh and dwelt among us. There is not a topic in Christendom or outside of Christendom more important than Jesus Christ.

There were specific prophecies in the Old Testament that Jesus Christ fulfilled in the New Testament. But the cool thing is, there are events that were established in times before Christ that were foreshadows of events that actually played out in real life in the life of Christ and to those around Him.

According to many scholars, Jewish and Gentile alike, there are over seventy major prophecies in the Old Testament relating to the coming Messiah, and each one would have to be fulfilled...exactly—for one to qualify as being the long-awaited Messiah. And consider the fact these prophecies were all in place 450–500 years before Christ was born. The odds of these prophecies being fulfilled by one person are absolutely astronomical. But Jesus did.

Born of a virgin (Isaiah 700–800 years B. C.)...check.

Born in Bethlehem (Micah 700–800 years B. C.)...check.

Betrayed for thirty pieces of silver (Zechariah 500 years B. C.)...check.

And many, many more. Enters Jerusalem on a donkey, garments divided by casting lots, abandoned by His followers, buried in a rich man's tomb, raised from the dead, and the list goes on. These are all Old Testament prophecies written centuries before, all fulfilled by one person, Jesus Christ. These prophecies from the Law, the writings, and the prophets come from what we call the Old Testament. The fascinating thing is that these are the prophecies identified as Messianic prophecies (prophecies directly relating to the coming Messiah) recognized by the Jewish scholars many hundreds of years before the time of Christ. This is what the Jews were waiting for, and it was the Jewish rabbis, many years before Jesus was born, who identified these as the signs of the coming Messiah. Jesus Christ fulfilled them all.

But there is another level of fulfillment, not necessarily prophetic in the same sense, but still prophetic and absolutely astounding just the same. Throughout the first five books of Moses, commonly known as "the Law," there are events that take place, certain rituals placed on the people and priests, and ceremonial requirements that have to happen. Through these events, Jesus Christ is in them all. This is the foreshadowing of Jesus Christ not only in ancient Scripture but in ancient Jewish tradition. And here, in these events, we see the Scriptures played out in real life, and the parties involved did not even realize they were taking part in a grand plan written long beforehand. I want to show you some hidden treasures of how God works through human events foreshadowing prophecies in real life through the person of Jesus Christ. It is my hope these things will show you the divine inspiration of the Holy Word of God since only God could orchestrate this across the millennia, and it then comes to pass exactly how He established it. I will start with a scripture and then tell the story of how it plays out. Let's start with Pontius Pilate.

Pontius Pilate and the Scapegoat

Leviticus 16:5–9 (NASB),
And he shall take from the congregation of the sons of Israel two male goats for a sin offering and one ram for a burnt offering. Then Aaron shall offer the bull for the sin offering which is for himself, that he may make atonement for himself and for his household. And he shall take the two goats and present them before the Lord at the doorway of the tent of meeting. And Aaron shall cast lots for the two goats, one lot for the Lord and the other lot for the scapegoat. Then Aaron shall offer the goat on which the lot for the Lord fell, and make it a sin offering.

Now, jump forward almost two thousand years from this verse in Leviticus, which says that when the priest makes this particular sacrifice, he shall come before the Lord with two goats—one to sacrifice, one to set free, which the Scriptures call the scapegoat.

Your name is Pontius Pilate, and unbeknownst to you, you are about to go down in history.

You literally have no idea you are taking part in a grand prophetic event that has been played out since the time of Moses that you are now front and center of.

You, Pilate, are standing in front of a throng of people who are clamoring for the blood of this preacher, this miracle worker. You realize that it was because of envy that He was delivered up to you by their religious leaders, but before you stands an itinerant preacher called Jesus Christ. You, as the Roman procurator of Judea, are not the least bit concerned about violations of their Jewish customs and laws; that is what they have their priests for. But it was the priests who delivered this man to you. This time they brought Him with a different charge—sedition. So now it involves Rome, and now you have to deal with it.

You interview this Jesus, and you ask Him, "Do You not hear how many things they testify against You?" And you are amazed that He gives no answers to the accusations. In fact, you find no fault in Him at all, and you go back to the crowd and tell them to take Him and judge Him according to their own law. But that would not suffice for them, so as an act of appeasement, you attempt to punish and release Him. But...they would not have it; they brought Him to you because they wanted you to condemn Him and put Him to death—and you can see that the priests and elders are stirring up the crowd. While sitting in your judgment seat, even your wife comes to you and says, "Have nothing to do with this righteous man,"[3] but the crowd is growing and getting out of control.

You realize this man is innocent; you actually say the words, "I find no fault in Him." He has done nothing deserving of death. You look for an out. They will not give you an out.

Then you remember you have a custom that as an act of goodwill, during the feast, you would release any one prisoner that they desired. And you were holding a notorious prisoner, one named Barabbas. This Barabbas was an insurrectionist, a robber, and a murderer. Certainly, the crowd...

So you ask them, "Whom shall I release to you? Jesus or Barabbas?"

The crowd cries out, "Give us Barabbas!"

"What shall I do with Jesus?"

"Crucify Him! Give us Barabbas!"

"Why? What evil has He done?" You are almost pleading, not wanting to send an innocent man to His death. So again, you tell the crowd, "I will therefore punish Him and release Him."

The crowd grows more insistent hurling comments like, "You are no friend of Caesar! His blood be on us and our children!"

You are left with no choice; a riot was starting, so you hand Jesus Christ, the Lamb of God, over to be crucified; Barabbas is set free. The ancient scripture has been fulfilled.

We have a scapegoat. Jesus is the sacrifice. Barabbas is the scapegoat, just as the scriptures in Leviticus say.

The Washing of Hands

You have given the Jewish leaders what they desired. You did not realize the vehemence of the crowd, nor did you realize that you were about to fulfill another scripture. After you release Barabbas and sentence Jesus to death, you wash your hands...

Leviticus 16:26 (NASB), "And the one who released the goat as the scapegoat shall wash his clothes and bathe his body with water."

Matthew 27:24 (NASB),
And when Pilate saw that he was accomplishing nothing, but rather that a riot was starting, he took water and washed his hands in front of the multitude, saying, "I am innocent of this Man's blood; see to that yourselves."

You did everything you could do to release an innocent man; it disgusts you that you were forced to release an actual criminal in His place.

Per Jewish law and custom, it fell to the high priest to administer the sacrifices in the temple. It was the chief priests and Sanhedrin (Jewish leaders and elders of the council) who brought Jesus Christ to Pilate. It was the high priest (Caiaphas) who brought the accusations to Pilate. Just as the duties of the high priest were to offer the lamb of sacrifice for the sins of the people, it is also the high priest who has selected Jesus Christ Jesus to be sacrificed, the ancient prophecy playing out in real life. Jesus of Nazareth is now the last true sacrifice ever selected by any high priest.

According to their law, the priests had to offer the sacrifice; no one else could do so, not even Pilate. The priests brought Jesus to Pilate to condemn Him, but the governor of Judea, a Gentile not under Jewish law, wanted no part of it. Pilate inspected Jesus, questioned Him, and found Him to be without fault. Prophetically speaking, Jesus Christ was without spot or blemish, just as it was required by Jewish law. Pontius Pilate tried to release Him; it was the priests who stirred up the mob. The Scriptures say that a riot was beginning, and that was what condemned Jesus. Pilate, seeing the mob getting out of control, was left with no choice; he had to hand Him over. But then Pilate does an interesting thing, he ceremonially washes his hands, declaring himself innocent. The sentence of death now falls back to the priests as they take their part in their fulfillment of Scripture. And again, Pilate unknowingly, as he washes his hands, plays out his own role in the fulfillment of ancient Scripture.

Old Times/New Times Converge

"Now the Lord said to Moses and Aaron in the land of Egypt, 'This month shall be the beginning of months for you; it is to be the first month of the year for you'" (Exodus 12:1-2, NASB).

The 1st of Nisan is an incredibly important day on the Hebrew calendar. Everything relating to *all* of the prophetic events surrounding the birth, death, and resurrection of Jesus Christ is connected to this day and begins with this month. Per Exodus 12, on Nisan 1, just before the Israelites embarked on their great Exodus from Egypt after 400 years of bondage, God Almighty spoke to Moses and rewrote the calendar. God told them this day would now be the first month of the year for them.

Then God told them that on the tenth day of this month, they were to each take a lamb for themselves, a lamb for each household. This is the first Hebrew day of observance ever given by God to Israel; way before Mount Sinai, before the ten commandments, even before Passover, this was the first day of observance, and the Jews called the 10th Nisan "Lamb Selection Day" or the "Day of the Lamb."[4]

The 10th day of Nisan became the day that each year, priests from the temple would travel to Bethlehem to select the lamb that would be ceremonially perfect according to the Scriptures; a male, a year old, without spot, without blemish, without defect, to be the sacrificial lamb for the Passover observance. This is the lamb that would be offered on the altar as a sin sacrifice which was representative of the sins of the people.

The date of Nisan 10 is important for other reasons also. Because during the time of Christ, on 10th Nisan, as the temple priests were traveling from the south on the way back from Bethlehem with their perfect lamb headed to Jerusalem, another Lamb—also born in Bethlehem, also perfect, without spot or blemish, was coming in from the east from Bethany on that very same day and He also entered Jerusalem. [5]

His name is Jesus Christ.

The day the sacrificial lamb came from Bethlehem to Jerusalem to cover the sins of the people is the same day Jesus entered Jerusalem on the back of a donkey. The Jews observed Lamb Selection Day; we call it Palm Sunday.

This day, Palm Sunday, when Jesus entered Jerusalem, begins what Christians around the world now call Holy Week—or Passion Week—as this is the final week before Jesus goes to the cross.

But back to the Old Testament, God told Moses and Aaron they were to bring the lamb into the household on the 10th day of Nisan and keep the lamb until the 14th day of the month. During those four days, the lamb became their lamb; they would have taken care of it, fed it, become attached, especially the kids, and made sure no harm came to it because at twilight on the 14th day of the month, they were to kill it—to sacrifice it—as part of the second holy day of observance ever given by God to the Israelites, a holy day known as Passover. This lamb represented a sin covering in their place, an ugly picture of the cost of sin. Sin is not free; the wages of sin is death. It happened with Adam and Eve when God clothed them in the garden, and it continued on down through the ages up to the time of Christ. God has always, out of His love, provided a substitutionary sacrifice on our behalf, but the price would always have to be paid. This sacrifice should mean something; it should cause pain and remorse; it was not supposed to be easy or taken lightly. A life was given up and was dying in your place. So you keep, nurture, and protect the lamb for four days. They knew this sacrifice was a covering for sin in their stead. The lamb is a sin offering, and the full punishment of sin went to the lamb, not to them.

On the very first Passover, once the lamb was sacrificed, they were told to take some of the blood and put it on the two doorposts and on the lintel of the house, which, ironically, makes a cross.

The hidden treasure is this: Just like the lamb was taken into the household for four days, Jesus of Nazareth also stayed four days in the Jerusalem area following His entry into Jerusalem. And just like the lamb taken into the household was inspected for spots and blemishes to make sure it was the perfect sacrifice, Jesus was also inspected by the religious leaders of His day. His entry to Jerusalem was followed by a cross-examination by the scribes, priests, and Pharisees for four days. So for the next few days, Jesus of Nazareth is busy, especially in the temple and the surrounding areas of Jerusalem, teaching, preaching, helping, and yes, even calling some people out, especially the religious leaders—Pharisees, Sadducees, scribes, elders, and lawyers. The religious leaders have come against Him and were seeking ways to destroy Him.

Monday through Wednesday of this week are packed with events that even a nominal churchgoer or Bible reader would recognize. Following His entry into Jerusalem on Sunday, it was on Monday morning that, while walking from Bethany to Jerusalem, Jesus cursed the barren fig tree, and it withered; and later gave the parable of the fig tree, symbolic of the future of Israel. Also, on this day, Jesus cleansed the temple, driving out the money changers, overturning the tables saying that "it shall be a house of prayer and you have made it a robbers' den."[6] He taught about the last days on the Mount of Olives, gave signs of His return, and told them to pay to Caesar what was Caesar's and to God what was God's. It was also during these few days that He told many of His parables, some in private to His disciples, some openly to the masses. Well-known parables such as the parable of the landowner, the parable of the marriage feast, the parable of the vine-growers, and many more. This was also when the Pharisees and religious leaders, upset at the growing popularity of Jesus, had had enough and joined together to try to ambush Jesus, trying to make Him slip in some matter of the Law with the intent of putting Him under arrest. While the common people were astonished at His teaching, the religious authorities were not so much. Many of the parables were aimed at the misguided hypocrisy of the Pharisees, which incensed them even more, and they conspired together to begin their plot to silence Him. The Sadducees jumped in and confronted Him about marriage in the afterlife, and Jesus silenced them, marveling to the people at their lack of understanding of the things of God as religious leaders.

And Jesus would, in turn, ask the religious leaders questions such as:

"The baptism of John—was it from heaven or from men?" (Luke 20:4, NKJV). The religious leaders could not answer Jesus because they were not followers of John; either answer would have gotten them in trouble because the people held John to be a prophet. They simply replied, "We don't know."

> And He said to them, "How is it that they say the Christ is David's son? For David himself says in the book of Psalms, 'THE LORD SAID TO MY LORD, "SIT AT MY RIGHT HAND, UNTIL I MAKE THINE ENEMIES A FOOT-

STOOL FOR THY FEET.'" "David therefore calls Him 'Lord,' and how is He his son?"

Luke 20:40–44 (NASB)

The religious authorities of the day, the religious rulers and teachers of the people, could not or would not answer this question.

It was also on this day that Jesus Christ of Nazareth actually wept over Jerusalem, wishing that they had recognized the time of their visitation.

Wednesday of Holy Week is a memorable day for two other reasons:

It was on Wednesday during this Passion Week that Judas made his bargain with the Jewish leaders to find an opportunity to betray Jesus.

It was Wednesday during Passion Week that Mary anointed the feet of Jesus in recognition of who He was.

Two people, two decisions, two destinies.

But We Must Beware the Leaven

It is amazing how Scripture plays out in real life. In the Scriptures, both Old and New Testaments, leaven represents sin. Even Jesus warned the people to "beware of the leaven of the Pharisees!" (Matthew 16:6, NASB).

During the time of Passover and the Feast of Unleavened Bread, not only are you not to eat anything with leaven, but leaven is not even to be found in your house.

This is a commandment of God that goes back to Exodus 12 to commemorate the day that God brought the Israelites out of Egypt.

Exodus 34:25 (NASB) says, "You shall not offer the blood of My sacrifice with leavened bread, nor is the sacrifice of the Feast of the Passover to be left over until morning." God was serious about leaven, and even today, observant Jews will search the house and remove any leaven from their homes during these times.

Jump forward almost two thousand years and place yourselves with Jesus and His disciples on the Thursday before His crucifixion when His disciples ask Jesus where they are to prepare for the Passover. Jesus told them that all was prepared and taken care of. This event which was a Jewish Passover[7] is what we know as the Last Supper. And since the Last Supper was a Passover meal, there can be no leaven.

Here is the hidden treasure: Jesus knew He was going to be betrayed that night; He knew that Judas was conspiring with the Jewish religious authorities and even told them so: He tells them they are clean, but not all of them. One is not clean. Jesus tells them, "He who dipped his hand with Me in the bowl is the one who will betray Me" (Matthew 26:23, NASB).

There is leaven; sin in the room.

Jesus then looks at Judas and tells him, "What you do, do quickly," and He sends Judas out to complete his task.

The final leaven has just been cleared from the room.

Enter the Cohanim

It seems there is always more than meets the eye; more depth, more meaning, and more to learn. For example, the Cohanim—members of the Jewish priesthood.

Everything that God does is exact and specific to the minutest detail. Everything He says is going to happen actually happens the way He says it will, even if we don't recognize it at the time. Sometimes, it is not just ceremonial events representing a sacred cause; it actually plays out in normal everyday life.

Enter the Cohanim.

Cohanim (Hebrew term for "priest"), simply stated, are the priests of Israel—but not just any priest. You cannot ask to become a priest, apply for the position, or volunteer; you had to actually be born into the priesthood.

The status of Cohanim was conferred upon Aaron, the brother of Moses, and to the generations of his sons by Almighty God during the great exodus two thousand years before Christ.[8] Aaron was a descendent of the tribe of Levi, who was one of the twelve sons of Jacob, by whom we get the twelve tribes of Israel. And God specifically set aside the tribe of Levi to be the priests for His people.[9] All priests were of the tribe of Levi; however, not all Levites were priests. It was a very specific and comparatively small group of people. Only male Levites descended from the line of Aaron could be priests...or Cohanim. Only the Cohanim could perform specific temple duties. Non-priest Levites (all those who descended from Levi, the son of Jacob, but not from Aaron) could have other temple ground roles, but only Levites descended from the line of Aaron could be priests.

It was the responsibility of the priests from the time of Aaron up until the destruction of the temple in 70 A.D. to observe the Tamid—the daily sacrifices in the temple, which took place every day at 9 a.m. and 3 p.m., and to oversee the daily functions of the temple and Jewish holy day observances (Passover, Yom Kippur, etc.).

It was the Cohanim who ministered in the temple, who were given charge by God over the offerings and the sacrifices, who identified and selected the lamb to be offered upon the altar, and it was the Cohanim who ensured to the people of Israel that the sacrifice was perfect and acceptable. At the command of Almighty God, these duties could not be performed by just anybody; they must be performed by the Cohanim, the descendants of both Levi and Aaron.

Ahhh, but what if there was one born of a lineage where both of his parents were descendants of both Levi and Aaron? This one would be special.

The hidden treasure is this: There was born to the Cohanim, to the house of Aaron, of the tribe of Levi, a child who was not only a priest but one descended from Aaron on both his father's and his mother's side;[10] he was a pure-blooded priest.

His name is John the Baptist.

Zacharias would have been at the end of the line of the Aaronic priesthood for his family because he and his wife Elizabeth were both advanced in age, and she was barren—that is, unless they had a son. The day came when he was chosen by lot[11] to perform his priestly service in the temple, for Zacharias, the father of John the Baptist, was Cohanim—and there he learned that God was about to produce one last priest.

Alone in the chamber performing his temple duties appears the angel Gabriel who tells Zacharias his petitions have been heard and that he is going to have a son and to name him John. When the time came for the birth of John, Zacharias, filled with the Holy Spirit,[12] prophesized about his son, "And you, child, will be called the prophet of the Most High" (Luke 1:76, NASB).

John the Baptist was both a priest and a prophet. He was, in fact, the last of the Old Testament prophets, for he was living in the old while proclaiming the new.

Filled with the Holy Spirit while yet in his mother's womb,[13] the angel tells Zacharias that John would be the forerunner of the Messiah to prepare the way for Him.

It was the temple priests, the Cohanim, who presented the lambs for sacrifice in the temple; it was John the Baptist who presented the Lamb Messiah, the final sacrifice to Israel.

It was John the Baptist who, when he saw Jesus, said to the masses, "Behold, the Lamb of God who takes away the sin of the world!" (John 1:29, NASB).

It was John the Baptist who said, "This is He on behalf of whom I said, 'After me comes a Man who has a higher rank than I, for He existed before me'" (John 1:30, NASB), even though John the Baptist was born about six months before Jesus.

It was John the Baptist, both priest and prophet, the scriptural Cohanim, who said, "I have seen, and have borne witness that this is the Son of God" (John 1:34, NASB).

But the Scriptures teach us that Jesus is also a high priest, a high priest of a different order. Rather than a priest of the order of Aaron, Jesus Christ, of the line of David, was a high priest of the order of Melchizedek,[14] the king of Salem, which later became Jerusalem. And like all priests, since the Law mandates that prior to beginning your priestly service, you are to be immersed in the ritual bath called a Mikveh,[15] this Jesus did, with John, when He was baptized in the river Jordan to begin His ministry.

Two priests representing two orders, one superseding the other, "In order to fulfill all righteousness."[16]

It is astonishing that the first declaration made to the Israelites outside the immediate family of Jesus was not given to the religious or political rulers of Israel but to simple shepherds keeping their flocks. And as it had been done since the time of Moses, the Cohanim had identified the lamb, the Cohanim had presented the lamb to the people and verified every requirement had been met; the lamb was perfect, without spot or blemish, born in Bethlehem, presented by a priest, and the ritual washing prior to starting sacred service was accomplished. John the Baptist knew that this was the Lamb of God that would take away the sins of the world.

Jesus Christ has met all of these scriptural, legal, and prophetic requirements. So far, all have been perfectly accomplished.

After John the Baptist baptized Jesus in the Jordan River, a voice from heaven answered, "Thou art My beloved Son, in Thee I am well-pleased" (Mark 1:11, NASB).

This was the acceptable sacrifice.

The Hidden Beauty of the Hyssop

Hyssop is a beautiful plant with remarkable meaning. In the Old Testament, the hyssop plant is mentioned several times; but it is mentioned just twice in the New Testament, and one of those mentions is in reference back to the Old Testament. Every time we see the hyssop plant in the Old Testament, it has to do with cleansing or the forgiveness of sins. In chapter fifty-one of the book of Psalms, King David uttered the following words, "Purify me with hyssop, and I shall be clean" (Psalm 51:7, NASB).

Ceremonially, the hyssop plant is used as part of the ritual in the atonement of sacrifices.

> As for the live bird, he shall take it, together with the cedar wood and the scarlet string and the hyssop, and shall dip them and the live bird in the blood of the bird that was slain over the running water.
> Leviticus 14:6 (NASB)

It was the plant the Israelites used to sprinkle blood on the door post the night of the exodus from Egypt, as we see in Exodus 12:22 (NASB), "And you shall take a bunch of hyssop and dip it in the blood which is in the basin, and apply some of the blood that is in the basin to the lintel and the two doorposts."

The above process of putting blood on the doorposts was given as part of the very first Passover when God, through Moses, brought the Israelites out of Egypt. When Moses went to Pharaoh and said, "Let My people go," after this night, Pharaoh let them go. God told them that the firstborn of all man and beast would die that night, with the exception of those that were under the blood. Taking the hyssop, dipping it in the blood of the basin, and using the hyssop to put the blood on the doorposts and lintel, puts the house under the blood. Remember, the blood came from the Passover lamb, and you could not leave the house or go outdoors until all was finished. You had to stay under the blood.

Leviticus 17:11 (NASB) puts it this way: "For the life of the flesh is in the blood, and I have given it you on the altar to make atonement for your souls; for it is the blood by reason of the life that makes atonement."

Cleansing and the Forgiveness of Sin

So, let's leave Moses for now and go forward again about two thousand years to the cross of Jesus Christ. Hyssop, as repeated over and over in the Old Testament, again plays a role in a sacrificial offering, but this time, it is with a different sacrificial lamb; it is in the last minutes with Jesus on the cross.

It is Passover—Jesus had already been tried and convicted by the Sanhedrin, He had been in front of Pilate, Herod, back to Pilate, been beaten, whipped, scourged, brought before the people, condemned, and carried His cross to Calvary. They have nailed Him to the cross, and He has been hanging there for almost six hours. In addition to all of the unspeakable physical sufferings He has endured while hanging on the cross, Jesus Christ is then mocked and ridiculed by the masses of people around Him. "He saved others, He could not save Himself," "Come down from the cross and we will believe You,"[17] the slurs themselves being a fulfillment of Scripture.

It is amazing when you realize you could be part of a greater plan when, unknowingly, through you, things are accomplished that God said long ago would happen.

For example, He was betrayed for thirty pieces of silver, a fulfillment of Zechariah 11; He was pierced through His hands and feet, a fulfillment of Zechariah 12; He was sneered and mocked, a fulfillment of Psalm 22; the soldiers who crucified Him cast lots for His clothing, a fulfillment of Psalm 22; a soldier pierced His side as He hung on the cross, a fulfillment of Zechariah 12; and He was crucified, tortured, suffered, "like a lamb that is led to the slaughter ...He would render Himself as a guilt offering" as found in Isaiah 53:7, 10 (NASB). No one who did these things to Jesus realized that they were taking their role in fulfilling prophetic events, which were written down millennia beforehand. Satan himself must have been in the crowd because one of the insults hurled at Jesus eerily harkens back to the beginning of Jesus' ministry when, after His baptism in the Jordan River, Jesus went into the wilderness where He fasted and prayed for forty days—and satan himself comes to Jesus and challenges Him on three occasions using these exact same words, "If you are the Son of God..."

when suddenly, at the cross, someone out in the crowd yells to Jesus, "If you are the Son of God—come down from the cross and we will believe You!"[18]

Jerusalem is packed with people because Passover is a high holy day, and many will pilgrimage from all over the land to come worship at the temple. Jesus has spent the last three years touching people all over the region. He healed the sick, brought sight to the blind, cleansed the lepers, and on more than one occasion, Jesus Christ raised the dead. To anyone, He would have been a prophet, or at the very least, someone that God was with or working through, for no man could have performed these signs on their own. Or...maybe He was something more. Maybe He was the Messiah. But on the day of His crucifixion, you would not have known it because of all of the many people He has touched, helped, healed, and taught throughout the region over the past three years; of His supporters, there are about five who remained with Him at the foot of the cross; four of them women. The rest of His followers have completely abandoned Him, their own fulfillment of Scripture, including His closest disciples, one of whom betrayed Him and one who denied Him. They all left Him—minus one. John. John was at the cross.

It is now almost 3 p.m. By now, you should know what this means—it is time for the priest to offer the evening sacrifice in the temple, the Tamid. But there is another sacrifice already taking place.

SALVATION, THE BAPTISM IN THE HOLY SPIRIT, AND THE GIFT OF TONGUES

We will pick up with John 19:28 (NASB), "After this, Jesus, knowing that all things had already been accomplished, in order that the Scripture might be fulfilled, said, 'I am thirsty.'"

A jar full of sour wine was standing there, so they put a sponge full of the sour wine *upon a branch of hyssop* and brought it up to His mouth.

When Jesus, therefore, had received the sour wine, He said, "It is finished!" and He bowed His head and gave up His spirit.

The same plant that the Israelites used to put blood on the doorposts, the plant that the Scriptures used for cleansing and forgiveness of sin, the same plant King David asked God to cleanse him with, has found its way to the cross.

As that hyssop branch makes its appearance in the Gospels, I am reminded of just why Jesus is on the cross. He is not there for anything He had done but for what you and I had done. His business is to cleanse us in the forgiveness of sins.

It was Passover. The Lamb was slain. It is finished; all of Scripture has been fulfilled; all of the requirements have been met down to the minutest detail, even down to the hyssop branch.

MICHAEL L. DAVIS

First Fruits, Feast Days, and Jesus Christ

For the Passover observance, two-thousand years before the time of Christ, God tells Moses and Aaron in Exodus 12 to bring the lamb into the household on the tenth day of the month of Nisan. Jesus entered Jerusalem on the 10th of Nisan, and on that same day, in obedience to Scripture, the priest entered Jerusalem from Bethlehem with the Passover lamb. As mentioned earlier, the Jews of the time called this day "The Day of the Lamb." We call it the Triumphal Entry and Palm Sunday.

The first observance ever given to the Israelites from God was on the 10th Nisan, found in Exodus 12 when the Lord told the Israelites to select the lamb. The next observance which would happen was on the 14th Nisan, which was the Feast of Passover, so called because this was when the angel of death would "pass over" any household that had the blood of the lamb on their doorposts. Immediately following Passover began the Feast of Unleavened Bread, which was a seven-day feast. But between Passover and the Feast of Unleavened Bread is another feast called First Fruits. First Fruits is an observance that falls on the day after the Sabbath following Passover. That is a lot; let me say that again: First Fruits is Jewish observance (feast) given to Moses by God that falls on the day after the Sabbath following the Passover. So you have Passover, then comes the Sabbath (Friday evening to Saturday evening), and the day following the Sabbath is First Fruits (Sunday). This is the first fruits of the harvest and was to be presented to the priests during the Feast of Unleavened Bread, and Israel may not eat the crops until the first fruits offering had been presented to the priests, and this begins the harvest time.

Jewish days and times are counted from sundown to sunset. Jesus Christ entered Jerusalem on Sunday, 10th Nisan. He had the last supper Thursday evening (after sundown, which by their calendar makes it Friday), was betrayed and arrested in the Garden of Gethsemane, stood before the Sanhedrin, stood before Pilate, Herod, then back to Pilate, and then crucified on the morning of Friday, 14th Nisan, the Passover. He was in the grave on Saturday, which is the Sabbath following Passover.

Here is the hidden treasure: Jesus Christ rose from the grave on Sunday, the day after the Sabbath (Saturday) following Passover (Friday). Jesus Christ rose from the grave on the feast day of First Fruits.

Even the apostle Paul, who many forget was not only a follower of Jesus Christ, but he was also a Jewish Pharisee, he knew the Scriptures, and he saw this as a fulfillment of Scripture because he wrote about it in 1 Corinthians 15:20 (NASB) when he said, "But now Christ has been raised from the dead, the first fruits of those who are asleep."

In fulfillment of the Scriptures, with the resurrection of Jesus Christ, the harvest has begun.

The Tamid

Two thousand years before the time of Christ and up to the year 70 A. D., the Israelites performed two sacrifices each day;[19] the morning lamb would be offered at the third hour of the day (9 a.m.) when, after the sacrifice, the trumpets would sound, and the temple gates would then be opened for prayers, commerce, and other religious events.

At the ninth hour (3 p.m.), the evening sacrifice was made and offered on the altar, at which time all of the offerings for the day would be finished.

Each day would begin with the sacrifice of the morning lamb and end with the sacrifice of the evening lamb. These sacrifices took place each day throughout the year. All of the other personal sacrifices and offerings that regular people would bring to the priests, such as goats, lambs, turtle doves, barley, etc., plus normal temple business would take place between those two sacrifices.

With the exception of a time period when the temple in Jerusalem was twice destroyed by invaders, from the time of Moses, in what was called the "tent of the meeting" (because it was an actual tent) up until the time of the first and second temples, and through the time of Christ, the temple sacrifices were performed daily, twice a day, every day of the week and were called the

Tamid, which is the perpetual sacrifice ordained by God to Moses.[20] The first daily sacrifice was at 9 a.m., and the second daily sacrifice was at 3 p.m.

The Gospels say it was the third hour when they crucified Jesus. That is 9 a.m.

The Gospels also say it was the ninth hour when He died. That is 3 p.m.

Here is the hidden treasure: Jesus Christ was nailed to the cross to begin the final sacrifice for all of humanity at the same time the priest entered the temple to present the morning offering.

Jesus died on the cross at the same time the priest was offering the evening sacrifice.

Jesus fulfilled the Tamid.

Only God could do this.

Only God could have had something written two thousand years before He Himself came to us and fulfilled it perfectly as He said it would be.

The Feast of the Fiftieth Day

We have touched on several of the Jewish holy feasts, such as Passover, First Fruits, and the Day of the Lamb, that were literally fulfilled in person by Jesus Christ. Have you heard of Shavuot?

Shavuot, one of the three major Jewish pilgrimage holidays, is the day celebrating when Moses went up to Mount Sinai to receive the ten commandments.

Shavuot is also the same day that after the resurrection of Jesus Christ, God pours out His Spirit on His church.

We call it Pentecost.

Shavuot means "weeks" and is sometimes called the Feast of Weeks and is directly linked to Passover because it comes fifty days after Passover.

Moses went up to Mount Sinai to receive the ten commandments from Almighty God, seven Sabbaths after the exodus from Egypt. The day before the exodus was Passover, the Israelites then left Egypt the following day, and seven Sabbaths later, Moses was on Mount Sinai trembling. The Bible calls it "a week of weeks," and it is fifty days after Passover.

Pentecost is the Hebrew Feast of Shavuot.

On Pentecost, Moses ascends Mount Sinai and returns with the Law.

On Pentecost, the Holy Spirit is poured out, and the church is born.

Acts 2:1 (NASB), "And when the day of Pentecost had come, they were all together in one place."

This was the 120 in the upper room where a sound came in like a rushing wind, those present were filled with the Holy Spirit, and tongues of fire were resting on them.

The same day the Law was given to Moses on the holy mountain is the same day—centuries later—God poured grace and truth to fulfill that very Law. It is the day the new covenant was empowered by God's Spirit and is exactly what John the Baptist was referring to when he said, speaking of Jesus, "I baptize you with water; but He will baptize you with the Holy Spirit" (Mark 1:8, NASB).

Look how the events of Jesus exactly coincide and fulfill the Jewish observance of the spring feasts: Jesus Christ entered Jerusalem on Palm Sunday (Day of the Lamb), He was crucified on what we call Good Friday (Passover), rose from the grave on what we call Easter (First Fruits), then fifty days later we celebrate the giving of the Spirit and the birth of the church on Pentecost (Shavuot).

Pentecost/Shavuot means the Spirit of God was given to believers on the same day the Law of God was given to Israel. When the Law was given, there was judgment. When the Spirit was given, there was grace. The spirit of the Law was replaced with the Spirit of truth.

It is interesting to note that in Exodus 33:28, after Moses came down the mountain with the ten commandments, he saw the Israelites in rebellion, saw the golden calf they had made, the anger of Moses burned, and the Bible says about 3,000 men fell that day. In Acts 2:40, when God poured out His Spirit, it says there were added to the church that day about 3,000 souls. So three thousand died, and centuries later, three thousand came to life on the exact same holy day. As the apostle Paul said, "The letter kills, but the Spirit gives life" (2 Corinthians 3:6, NASB).

Which brings me to another point. Pentecost is also a celebration of the spring harvest, which began fifty days earlier on the Feast of First Fruits, which, as we discussed, is the Sunday after the Sabbath after Passover. Fifty days after the Feast of First Fruits starts the countdown to the Feast of Weeks, or Pentecost, which was the grand celebration at the end of the grain harvest. All of this began in the time of Moses and is still observed today.

But somewhere around A. D. 33, the First Fruits of an even greater harvest issued forth, for it was on the first day after the Sabbath that occurred in the midst of the Passover celebration that Jesus rose from the dead. Lest there be any doubt that His resurrection fulfilled the Feast of First Fruits, Paul tells us explicitly that Christ is the first fruits of those who will be raised from the dead (1 Corinthians 15:20–23).

The harvest was ripe, for, on the day of Pentecost day after the resurrection of Jesus Christ, He added the first 3,000 souls to the church, the harvest of many to come.

The New Covenant and Substitutionary Sacrifice

Preface: A covenant is a relationship in which two parties make a binding promise to each other. There are several types of covenants, but the most sacred covenant is the blood covenant because it involves the sacredness of life. In ancient Jewish life, it was actually called "cutting" a covenant because it involved the cutting of a sacrifice. This Abraham did in Genesis 15. The Jewish sacrifices in the temple were part of the ongoing covenant. Both the old and new covenants are blood covenants. The terms "testament" and "covenant" imply the same meaning; however, what we call the Old Testament is not simply a list of books in the Bible before the time of Christ, nor is the New Testament simply a list of books following the time of Christ. It is more accurately defined as the history of God in how He dealt with the generations of the Israelites, and later the church, through the covenants which He has established. The Old Testament is the old covenant; the New Testament is the new covenant. Both involve the sacredness of life.

God has always worked through covenants. From the very beginning of human history, and by this, I am referring to as far back as Adam and Eve in the Garden of Eden. God has always worked with His creation through covenants. Without getting into a lot of theological depth, the premise, which has remained true since the beginning of time, is this: God is our creator, and He is a God of love. But He is also holy, and those that are in His presence must be clean and holy also. Part of His angelic creation found this out when a third of them rebelled, and God cast them out of heaven;[21] they could no longer be in His presence (the leader of the rebellion was Lucifer, who became satan, and the others who followed him are his demons).

But mankind is different; we were created in God's image. Angels were not, animals were not, only us. And the fact that we were created in God's image makes us special to God in all of His creation. In short, God Almighty took on human flesh in the person of Jesus Christ to reconcile us back to Him so we could spend eternity with Him. That makes us pretty special.

So, we all know the story of Adam and Eve and how they fell from grace in the Garden of Eden. They had a perfect face-to-face relationship with God—until they disobeyed His one commandment: do not eat from the tree of the knowledge of good and evil. Well, they did, and when they did, they introduced sin into the equation. Sin, simply speaking, is disobedience to God. God told them that the day they ate of the fruit of the tree, they would die. And when they did from the tree, they did die; first, spiritually, because the face-to-face relationship with God was broken, and later they died physically.

Why would God not want them to eat of the tree? It is so simple—God just wanted them to follow Him. God created us with free will, free to love a God of love, not a love that is coerced, and that is best expressed when that love is freely given—like Christ on the cross.

John 3:16 (NASB), "For God so loved the world, that He gave His only begotten Son." That kind of love—freely given. Well, Adam and Eve didn't need to learn about good and evil, for they were in a perfect relationship with God, free to obey, and if they simply followed God, it would all be good. In fact, it would be great. But they were also free to choose to go the other way, were deceived, and satan (leader of the fallen angels) lied and told Eve that "you surely shall not die! For God knows that in the day you eat from it your eyes will be opened, and you will be like God, knowing good and evil."[22] So she ate, Adam ate, and the rest is history. Man, we were so close...

Here is where the covenant part comes in. When they fell, the Bible says their eyes were opened, and they saw they were naked. So they hid, then they sewed fig leaves together to make a covering—it was, in essence, a covering to hide their sin. It didn't work, but this is the same as us trying to cover our own sin by our own ability—they call it fig leaves; we call it excuses. And in many respects, we call it religion—there are so many religions based on the premise that trying to be good or make amends by our own ability is sufficient instead of doing things God's way. So we compare ourselves to our neighbors or each other and come up with all of these religions, systems, and philosophies without realizing that there is only one standard—and that standard is to be perfect (without sin)—and we are not perfect. And Adam and Eve were perfect—until they weren't. So they disobeyed God, and they sinned.

But remember God said that when they disobeyed, there would be death involved?

Genesis 3:21 (NASB), "And the Lord God made garments of skin for Adam and his wife, and clothed them."

The Lord God took the skin of an animal and clothed Adam and Eve. Something had to die—to shed its blood—to cover the sin of Adam and Eve. This cost a life. There was death. Since their creation, this was probably the first time Adam and Eve had ever seen death. So right from the beginning, we see this principle of substitutionary sacrifice—which will go from Adam and Eve all the way to Jesus Christ.

Leviticus 17:11 (NASB), "For the life of the flesh is in the blood, and I have given it to you on the altar to make atonement for your souls; for it is the blood by reason of the life that makes atonement."

Hebrews 9:22 (NASB), "And without shedding of blood there is no forgiveness."

Adam and Eve then taught substitutionary sacrifice to their children, Cain and Abel. They were taught that the penalty for sin is death, but God has provided a means to meet that penalty. We all know the story of Cain and Abel, when they brought their offerings to the Lord, and how the Lord had regard for Abel's offering, but He rejected Cain's. Did you ever wonder why He rejected Cain's offering?

Let's look at Cain and Abel's offering:

Genesis 4:3–5 (NASB),

> So it came about in the course of time that Cain brought an offering to the Lord of the fruit of the ground. And Abel, on his part also brought of the firstlings of his flock and of their fat portions. And the Lord had regard for Abel and for his offering; but for Cain and for his offering He had no regard.

Abel brought the firstlings of his flock, his very best, and offered them on the altar. Cain brought the fruit of the ground. There was no blood; there was no substitutionary sacrifice. There was no covering for sin. This is why his was rejected. Cain tried to get by with something else; he tried to do this his own way because he did not want to do it God's way. He brought his second best and did not bring what was required.

We also know that substitutionary sacrifice was passed down through the generations to Noah. What was the first thing Noah did after the flood when he got off the ark?

Genesis 8:20 (NASB), "Then Noah built an altar to the Lord, and took of every clean animal and of every clean bird and offered burnt offerings on the altar."

And it was passed down from Noah to Abraham, Isaac, and Jacob, all through their descendants on down to Moses. Down through Bible history, altars were built to give offerings of thanksgiving and memorials of good things God has done.

This is called a covenant. Not just any covenant, it is the most sacred kind called a blood covenant. Sacred because a blood covenant represents a promise based on life because, as the Scriptures say, the life of the flesh is in the blood.

God cuts a covenant with Abraham and declares the promise would come from his descendants.[23] Over time, He reveals more and expands the scope of the covenant through seasons and feasts and establishes high holy days which are to be recognized. This blood covenant, which started with Adam and Eve, is carried down through Abraham and his sons. Over time, the priesthood was established during the time of Moses to administer the covenant, and the worship and sacrifice were made in a large tabernacle (tent) until King Solomon, King David's son, built a temple in Jerusalem. And a lot happens, a lot takes place through time and history, but through the disobedience of the Israelites, Jerusalem is ransacked, and the temple is destroyed for a time, and rebuilt, then rebuilt again in grandeur by King Herod.

This temple, from the time of Solomon until the time of King Herod, is where the old covenant was administered.

But even though this began in the very beginning with Adam and Eve, the old covenant was temporary and was already passing away. Way back in Genesis chapter 3, God was already planning on the Messiah, and down through history, the Israelites were waiting for His arrival. They looked to the writings and the prophets for indications of His revealing.

One of these prophets was named Jeremiah. He worked for God about 600 years before the time of Christ and was around during the destruction of Jerusalem. He was known as the "weeping prophet" because of all the warnings he would give to turn back to the true and living God, but they would not listen. Jeremiah knew it would bring destruction, and he wept over his people and his city.

Here is the hidden treasure; here is the kicker: God, speaking through Jeremiah, says the following:

> "Behold, days are coming," declares the Lord, "when I will make a new covenant with the house of Israel and with the house of Judah, not like the covenant which I made with their fathers in the day I took them by the hand to bring them out of the land of Egypt, My cov-

enant which they broke, although I was a husband to them," declares the Lord. "But this is the covenant which I will make with the house of Israel after those days," declares the Lord, "I will put My law within them, and on their heart I will write it; and I will be their God, and they shall be My people."

Jeremiah 31:31–33 (NASB)

The days were coming, said the prophet Jeremiah, about 600 years before Christ, that there would be a new covenant.

Fast forward, and let's join Jesus of Nazareth with His disciples at the Last Supper.

We will pick up at Luke 22:15,

And He said to them, "I have earnestly desired to eat this Passover with you before I suffer; for I say to you, I shall never again eat of it until it is fulfilled in the kingdom of God." And when He had taken a cup and given thanks, He said, "Take this and share it among yourselves; for I say to you, I will not drink of the fruit of the vine from now on until the kingdom of God comes." And when He had taken some bread and given thanks, He broke it, and gave it to them, saying, "This is My body which is given

for you; do this in remembrance of Me." And in the same way He took the cup after they had eaten, saying, "This cup which is poured out for you is the new covenant in My blood."
Luke 22:15–20 (NASB)

This is the new covenant.

This is the New Testament.

It is a blood covenant, a blood testament.

This is Jesus Christ, God in the flesh, who is our substitutionary sacrifice; from the time of Adam and Eve, God has been giving us glimpses and pictures all through history until the day would come when He would fulfill all of His promises on the cross. For the life of the flesh is in the blood; without the shedding of blood, there is no forgiveness. Not the blood of goats or lambs, but His own blood. He is the perfect sacrifice.

The New Testament book of Colossians, written by the apostle Paul, sums it up this way: "For He delivered us from the domain of darkness, and transferred us to the kingdom of His beloved Son, in whom we have redemption, the forgiveness of sins" (Colossians 1:13–14, NASB). He then goes further and says in the same book: "Having canceled out the certificate of debt consisting of decrees against us ...He has taken it out of the way, having nailed it to the cross" (Colossians 2:14, NASB).[24]

In Him, we have redemption through His blood and the forgiveness of sins, according to the riches of His grace. So says Ephesians 1:7. This is the new covenant.

The Cockcrow

"Then he began to curse and swear, 'I do not know the man!' And immediately a cock crowed" (Matthew 26:74, NASB).

"But Peter said, 'Man, I do not know what you are talking about.' And immediately, while he was still speaking, a cock crowed. And the Lord turned and looked at Peter" (Luke 22:60–61, NASB).

Maybe it's not like we have always seen it in the movies. You know, where Jesus is standing there in the wee hours of the morning being interrogated, but at this juncture, the camera is focusing on Peter, following fearfully at a distance, maybe warming himself by the fire, when he gets confronted one last time, everybody watching the movie knows it's coming, Peter makes his third and final denial of Jesus, and then it happens...off in the distance, a cock crows.

But maybe, just maybe, it was not a rooster at all. Consider this:

Within the twenty-four hours of the day, divisions of the day were broken down into hours, twelve hours for the day and twelve hours for the night. These were further broken down into "watches," four watches for the day and four watches for the night as follows:

Day Watches	Evening Watches
First watch, 6 am–9 am	First watch, 6 am–9 pm
Second watch, 9 am–12 pm	Second watch, 9 pm–12 am
Third watch, 12 pm–3 pm	Third watch, 12 am–3 am
Fourth watch, 3 pm–6 pm	Fourth watch, 3 am–6 am

So, for example, where the Gospel of Matthew says in chapter 27, verse 45 (NASB), "Now from the sixth hour darkness fell upon all the land until the ninth hour," that would be from noon to 3 p.m. Where the Gospel of Mark (15:25) says that Jesus was crucified at the third hour— that would be 9 a.m.

The Jewish day began at sundown, but what drove the divisions of the days was the Tamid (perpetual) sacrifice[25] that we discussed earlier. Remember that the Jewish temple conducted two sacrifices each day; one at 9 a.m. and one at 3 p.m.

Back to the watches...during the night watch, to signal the end of the third watch and the beginning of the fourth watch, there was a trumpet call that came from the temple. Do you know what this trumpet call was called that signaled the end of the third watch and the beginning of the fourth watch?

This trumpet call was called "Kerot Hagever," which translated means "cockcrow," or the call of the cock. At cockcrow, a cock crier would blow the trumpet signaling the change of the temple guards.

So what did Peter hear? Was it a rooster, or was it a trumpet? I don't know, I wasn't there, but I do know this: the Mishnah, the earliest compilation of rabbinic oral law, states that roosters (chickens) may not be raised in Jerusalem due to purity concerns (Mishna Bava Kama 7.7; see also b. Bava Kama 82b).[26] This decree came from the first century when the temple stood in Jerusalem. "They do not breed cocks at Jerusalem because of the holy things; as it is interpreted, cocks turn up dung hills, and set free the reptiles by which the sacrifices might be polluted."

Mishna Bava Kama 7:7 reads as such (emphasis mine):

> One may not raise chickens in Jerusalem, due to the sacrificial meat that is common there. There is a concern that chickens will pick up garbage that imparts ritual impurity and bring it into contact with sacrificial meat, thereby rendering it ritually impure. And priests may not raise chickens anywhere in Eretz Yisrael, because of the many foods in a priest's possession that must be kept ritually pure.

SALVATION, THE BAPTISM IN THE HOLY SPIRIT, AND THE GIFT OF TONGUES

I guess that Peter could have heard a rooster from somewhere outside of Jerusalem. Or maybe it was a rogue rooster, or maybe it was just like we see in the movies. But personally, I think that after the Last Supper, and after the Garden of Gethsemane, and after Judas betrayed Him, and it was now getting late, somewhere around 3 a.m., Peter was watching from a distance as Jesus was standing before Caiaphas and the Sanhedrin, when, after his last denial, Peter heard a cock crow.[27]

A Few Last Thoughts

I had an old buddy named Jim, and we were good friends; we knew and worked together for close to twenty-five years. We were not just friends and co-workers; we were brothers in the faith. Now, there were a few things we saw differently, nothing of core doctrinal significance, but still enough to share and have fun with each other. One of those topics was "the rapture." He was all in on the pre-trib theory, while I had a little different view. Another topic was actually about this one, the baptism in the Holy Spirit and (to him) the issue of tongues. At times we would go back and forth and round and round on these and other topics, quite actually enjoying each other's fellowship over the conversations.

One day, I am sitting at work, thinking about one of our previous discussions, so I send him an email:

Me: "Jim, you were right; it was pre-trib! Man, it is great up here! Wish you were here!"

He replied back something like, "jkdfdjeiujcjekek."

I emailed him back, "What is that?"

He said, "I was typing in tongues."

Oh man, I cracked up. That, to me, was hilarious, but that was the brotherhood and friendship we shared.

I have attempted to show why a certain part of the body of Christ believes and practices their faith the way they do. If a particular group or denomination absolutely rejects this and says the days of spiritual gifts have passed, they are called cessationists (gifts have ceased). If they belong to a denomination that was founded with this dogma, they are called Pentecostals—meaning their particular denomination was founded with the belief that the things which happened on the day of Pentecost and throughout the book of Acts and taught in the epistles are still with us today. If someone adheres to this doctrine but belongs to another denomination that does not formally recognize this as part of their church doctrine (Baptist, Episcopal, Catholic, Lutheran, etc.), they are called Charismatics—meaning they believe the gifts (charisma), which belonged to the early church, still belong to the church today. There are Charismatics spread out among all of the denominations that have received baptism in the Holy Spirit. They have discovered that all of the denominational arguments fall short, sought the Lord about it, and were blessed and filled. This does not make one more or less saved, but it does avail that person for so much more for what the Lord wants to offer.

I would like to point out that I realize there is abuse around the utilization of spiritual gifts. Not all that goes on is of God. These things are abused, flaunted, faked, sensationalized, commercialized, and marketed for profit. It takes discernment. I know there are fakes and forgeries out there. I know the fakes and forgeries give the rest a bad name. That is not of God. But that does not negate the true gifts that are from God. That does not cancel out what is true and real and from God. And I know some true gifts are misused today just as they were in Corinth. Anytime people get involved with anything God wants to do, it will get messed up just because people are involved. Examples of this are all through the Bible. Just ask Balaam. But the beauty of it is that God will still move among His people.

The measure of a person's spirituality is not by the gifts but by the fruits.

But at the same time, it should not be a person's goal just to speak in tongues. That should never be the focus. The focus is always on following Jesus. Speaking in tongues, whether as a private prayer language or a ministerial gift, does not mean you have "arrived;" the focus should be on Jesus Christ and serving Him. Our focus should be on the giver of the gifts, not the gifts themselves. Nor should a person think to himself or herself that they want everything God has for them except the tongues. I have often heard people say things like that before. They even admit that they believe in the baptism in the Holy Spirit and everything that goes with it, but they do not want the tongues.

I have heard people say, "If God wants me to have this, then He is just gonna have to do it, but I'm not asking for it." Well, let me ask you this: Is that how you got saved? Did you just say, "Well, if God wants me saved, He is just gonna have to do it"? Once again, our focus should be on Jesus; He died for us, He shed His blood for us, He rose again for us, and it is because of Him that we have the right to be called "children of the Most High God." We should desire whatever He has for us because He equips us to serve Him. Our focus should be on Jesus. And the same goes for the other side—if you are in the opposite camp, yet this is the main thing that you focus on, your focus needs to be Jesus as well.

But some will never believe or accept the baptism in the Holy Spirit. And that is okay. You do not have to accept it. You can be a born-again Christian without the fullness of the Holy Spirit. This has nothing to do with one's salvation. It does have to do with prayerfully striving for everything God has for us. And in reality, none of us fully achieve that. We will all miss the mark. That is why we have an intercessor and a Savior. Listen, we, as a body, need to be sensitive to the Holy Spirit in reaching people for Christ, touching people, helping people, and ministering to those who do not know Him. This is who we are. Followers of Christ.

On the day of Pentecost in Acts 2, Peter stood up and explained to the crowd that the miracle they were seeing was a fulfillment of prophecy from the prophet Joel, where he said the Spirit would be poured out in the last days. Are the last days over? We saw that praying in the Spirit was part of the armor of God listed in Ephesians. Why would God take part of our armor away? Was that just for the early church? Do we not need the same armor today? Romans 11:29 says that the gifts and the calling of God are irrevocable.

I once heard a preacher say, "When you get saved, that is all of the Holy Ghost you will ever get." I do not understand this. I do not understand how you can take our eternal God and limit Him to a box so small. Who is he to say that? In several places in the books of Acts, Luke mentions where the same disciples were filled over and over with the Holy Spirit. This was never intended to be a one-time event but an ongoing way of life for followers of Christ. I think it is sad that as children of God, the body of Christ would turn away from any gift the Lord would bestow upon us. We should desire anything from the Lord He wants us to have. This is for His service and for His glory. I would submit to you that it is not the gifts that have left the church; it is the church that has left the gifts.

Jesus said in Luke 5:37 that you do not put new wine into old wineskins; otherwise, the wineskins would burst. But you put new wine into new wineskins, and both are preserved. You are the wineskin, and the Holy Spirit is the wine. Get a new wineskin. Get born again. Then get filled with the Holy Spirit. Put some new wine into new wineskins. This is what God wants for you.

But I also wanted to show you that this Christian walk is not centered on this topic of spiritual gifts; it is about the preeminence of Jesus Christ and what He has done for us. This is critically important. It is about our Almighty God, the creator of the universe who loves us so much that He came to us in the form of a man to give His life as a ransom for us, that He took our punishment upon Himself to draw us to Him. He loves us that much.

And He loves you that much.

I wanted to show you that His Word, the Holy Bible testifies all throughout both the Old and New Testaments that He is who He said He is, for none of those things we discussed, the fulfillment of prophecy and the events that took place, could have happened except that God was in them, that God orchestrated them, and that God fulfilled them.

Only God could have done this because any rational person would have to admit that the probability of these events taking place on their own and being fulfilled exactly as they were is absolutely astronomical. I included those to show you that God is real, that God loves you, and that God wants you to be with Him for all eternity. He did this for you.

If you are a born-again believer and want to be equipped and empowered to serve the Lord in a greater capacity, the baptism in the Holy Spirit is waiting for you. I would encourage you to prayerfully seek the Lord about this.

If you are not a born-again Christian, I would ask that the Lord would use this discussion to bring you to a place of trusting Jesus Christ as your Lord and Savior; and then to receive the fullness of the blessings He has for your life. At any moment, you have the power to say, "This is not how my story will end."

Meet Jesus.

Get baptized in the Holy Spirit.

Go serve the Lord.

Amen.

About the Author

Having been raised in the faith and knowledge of God through several Christian traditions, Michael personally asked Jesus Christ into his life in 1974 as a fourteen-year-old teenager. After being born again, Michael met Jesus Christ again as his baptizer in the Holy Spirit as a young man in 1983. If you have questions, you can reach the author by email at *BibleDiscoveryWithMike@gmail.com*, and please put the word "Bible Question" in the subject line.

Endnotes

1. See Mark 1:3, John 1:23, and Luke 3:4
2. Genesis 2:17
3. Matthew 27:19
4. Called Korban Pesach, this term has the connotation of "approaching or nearness of sacrifice." This first Hebrew day of observance is given in Exodus 12:3.
5. Matthew 21:1; Mark 11:1; Luke 19:28
6. See Matthew 21:10
7. John 13:27
8. Exodus 28:1
9. Deuteronomy 10:8
10. Luke 1:5–8
11. Priestly duties were conducted year round by family division, and then by casting lots. Mishna Tamid 3:1 describes some of the duties determined by lot. Mishna Yoma 2 speaks to the temple duties determined by lot. The incense, attended to by Zacharias is mentioned in Yoma 2:4. King David divided the descendants of Levi into smaller divisions so that each family would have an equal opportunity to minister. Likewise, the priests were also divided. There were twenty-four divisions, which allowed each division, or order, to serve for two weeks each

year (1 Chronicles 24:4–6). The order of Abijah from whence Zacharias belonged, was the eighth order (verse 10).
12 Luke 1:67
13 Luke 1:15
14 cf: Psalm 110:4 and Hebrews 7:1–26
15 Exodus 29:4, Exodus 40:12 and the ritual is followed to this day.
16 See Matthew 3:15
17 See Matthew 27:40, 42
18 Matthew 27:40
19 This daily sacrifices, called The Tamid, was instituted with Moses and the Jewish nation as the perpetual sacrifice ordained by God in the book of Exodus. The Tamid has its own place in the Mishna portion of the Talmud. Talmud Mishna Tamid 1:2 through Tamid 4 reference the specific times and states the necessary rituals for conducting the two daily sacrifices (Tamid). Also see Flavius Josephus, first century Jewish historian, in *Antiquities of the Jews* 14.4.3 who stated, "The priests were not at all hindered from their sacred ministrations, by their fear during the siege, but did still twice each day, in the morning and about the ninth hour, offer their sacrifices on the altar."
20 Tamid (daily burnt offerings) instituted by God in Exodus 29:38, Numbers 23:8, and explained in Mishna Kodashim Tamid 1, chapters 1–7.
21 Isaiah 14:12; Luke 10:8; Hebrews 12:22; Revelation 9:1; Revelation 12:3
22 Genesis 3:1–5. Satan actually told Adam and Eve that they would be like God.
23 Genesis 15 gives an excellent narrative of what it is to "cut a covenant."
24 Colossians 2:13–14

25 See especially Mishna Sukkah 5:4.
26 Mishna Bava Kama 7 forbids the raising of roosters, chicken, or fowl in Jerusalem due to desecration.
27 References: Mishna Tamid 1:2 states the superintendent of the temple did not always come at the same time, "sometimes at cockcrow, sometimes a little later," and refers to a time in the early morning when the priests would prepare the temple for daily service. See also Mishna Yoma 1:8.